"Michael Card brilliantly leads as he gives language to this virtually undefinable word. When he first shared with me his basic definition of hesed—'When the person from which I have a right to expect nothing gives me everything'— I couldn't wait to learn more. I've been completely moved by this book: first, to explore and experience an aspect of God's character I never knew before, and second, to let his hesed inspire me to live hesed every day."

Ginny Owens, singer and songwriter

"Michael approaches the rich concept of God's hesed love from many different angles. The result is an edifying collection of reflections on the shocking, loyal, and limitless love of God in Christ for us and the world. Read it and you will not only learn but sing hesed!"

Jonathan Dodson, lead pastor of City Life Church, author of *Here in Spirit*

"Michael Card has given his life to joining the wonder of Scripture with careful scholarship. He writes with the touch of an artist, the mind of a scholar, the heart of a pastor, and the reverence of a disciple. This book, focused on the character of a merciful God, is not just a book about words in Scripture—it is a thoughtful, beautiful meditation on the Word Incarnate himself, Jesus Christ. A wonderful book."

Russ Ramsey, pastor, author of the Retelling the Story Series

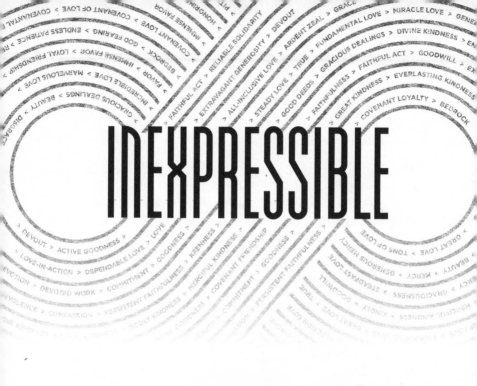

INEXPRESSIBLE

HESED
AND THE MYSTERY
OF GOD'S
LOVINGKINDNESS

MICHAEL CARD

IVP Books
An imprint of InterVarsity Press
Downers Grove, Illinois

InterVarsity Press
P.O. Box 1400, Downers Grove, IL 60515-1426
ivpress.com
email@ivpress.com

InterVarsity Press® is the book-publishing division of InterVarsity Christian Fellowship/USA®, a movement of students and faculty active on campus at hundreds of universities, colleges, and schools of nursing in the United States of America, and a member movement of the International Fellowship of Evangelical Students. For information about local and regional activities, visit intervarsity.org.

All Scripture quotations, unless otherwise indicated, are taken from the Christian Standard Bible®, copyright © 2017 by Holman Bible Publishers. Used by permission. Christian Standard Bible® and CSB® are federally registered trademarks of Holman Bible Publishers.

While any stories in this book are true, some names and identifying information may have been changed to protect the privacy of individuals.

Cover design: David Fassett
Interior design: Jeanna Wiggins
Images: gold background: © studiocasper / E+ / Getty Images
smoke: © Jose A. Bernat Bacete / Getty Images
blue abstract: © Khaneeros / iStock / Getty Images Plus

ISBN 978-0-8308-4549-1 (print)
ISBN 978-0-8308-7381-4 (digital)

Printed in the United States of America ∞

InterVarsity Press is committed to ecological stewardship and to the conservation of natural resources in all our operations. This book was printed using sustainably sourced paper.

Library of Congress Cataloging-in-Publication Data
Names: Card, Michael, 1957- author.
Title: Inexpressible : Hesed and the mystery of God's lovingkindness / Michael Card.
Description: Downers Grove : InterVarsity Press, 2018. | Includes bibliographical references and index.
Identifiers: LCCN 2018039220 (print) | LCCN 2018044415 (ebook) | ISBN 9780830873814 (eBook) | ISBN 9780830845491 (pbk. : alk. paper)
Subjects: LCSH: God (Christianity)—Love—Biblical teaching. | Kindness—Biblical teaching. | ̀Hesed (The Hebrew word)
Classification: LCC BT140 (ebook) | LCC BT140 .C267 2018 (print) | DDC 231/.6—dc23
LC record available at https://lccn.loc.gov/2018039220

P	21	20	19	18	17	16	15	14	13	12	11	10	9	8	7	6	5
Y	35	34	33	32	31	30	29	28	27	26	25	24	23	22	21	20	19

**WITH ENORMOUS
GRATITUDE AND AFFECTION**

this book is dedicated to

Dr. John Long,

a true hasid

HESED

LOVE, LOVINGKINDNESS, MERCIFUL LOVE, LOYAL LOVE, SURE LOVE, RELENTLESS LOVE, ENDURING LOVE, EXTRAVAGANT LOVE, AFFECTIONATE SATISFACTION, LOVE IN ACTION, DEPENDABLE LOVE, STEADY LOVE, TRUE LOVE, FUNDAMENTAL LOVE, MIRACLE LOVE, GENEROUS LOVE, DEEP LOVE, WONDERFUL LOVE, GREAT LOVE, INCREDIBLE LOVE, MARVELOUS LOVE, GRACIOUS LOVE, LOYAL IN LOVE, STEADFAST LOVE, EXPRESSION OF LOVE, ELECTION LOVE, UNFAILING LOVE, FAITHFUL LOVE, TONS OF LOVE, LOVING INSTRUCTION, LOVING DEEDS, COVENANT LOVE, COVENANT OF LOVE, COVENANTAL FAITHFULNESS, COVENANTAL DEEDS OF LOVE, COVENANT FRIENDSHIP, COVENANT COMMITMENT, GRACIOUS COVENANT, LOYAL, LOYALTY, COVENANT LOYALTY, LOYAL FAITHFULNESS, GREAT LOYALTY, UNSWERVING LOYALTY, LOYAL MERCY, LOYAL SERVICE, KINDNESS, KINDLY, DIVINE KINDNESS, LOYAL KINDNESS, GODLY KINDNESS, MERCIFUL KINDNESS, GREAT KINDNESS, EVERLASTING KINDNESS, MERCY, MERCY WORK, MERCY FEELING, MIRACLE MERCY, GENEROUS MERCY, BENEVOLENCE, COMPASSION, PERSISTENT FAITHFULNESS, FAITHFULNESS, FAITHFUL ACT, RELIABLE SOLIDARITY, GOODWILL, ARDENT ZEAL, GRACE, GRACIOUSNESS, EXTRAVAGANT GENEROSITY, LARGESSE, GLORY, HONOR, HONORING, PITY, CLEMENCY, ROCK, BEDROCK, GOD FEARING, PIETY, CHARITY, STRENGTH, DEVOUT, ACTIVE GOODNESS, FAVOR, IMMENSE FAVOR, LOYAL FRIENDSHIP, GOOD HEARTEDNESS, IMMENSE FAVOR, WORKING GRACIOUSLY, GENEROUS YES, ENDLESSLY PATIENT, GENEROUS ACT OF GOODNESS, DEVOTION, DEVOTED WORK, COMMITMENT, GOODNESS, GOOD DEEDS, GRACIOUS DEALINGS, BEAUTY, DISGRACE, REPROACH, SHAMEFUL THING, WICKED THING, STICK WITH ME, STICKING BY, STICKING WITH, BIG-HEARTEDNESS, "UNLIMITED, UNCONDITIONAL, UNCONDITIONED, AND ALL-INCLUSIVE LOVE FOR ALL CREATION"

CONTENTS

PREFACE

THE UNTRANSLATABLE DEFINING THE INEXPRESSIBLE

The most profound mysteries are not hidden away in remote, secret places; they are mostly an unrecognized part of everyday life. We fret over mowing the lawn and miss the deep mystery of how the grass grows. We seek to shush a weeping baby but rarely ask where tears come from and what they could possibly mean.

Most mysterious of all are the sounds we make with our teeth and tongue, the symbols we scratch across a legal pad and peck out on a keyboard. They seem the most ordinary part of our world—words— but they are a mystery. At this moment I am writing them and you are reading them; the thoughts that my words elicit in your brain are composed of words. In fact, we couldn't even think without them.

This book is founded on this inexpressible mystery in general and on perhaps the most mysterious and inexpressible word of all, the Hebrew word *hesed*.

THE WAY WORDS WORK

The discussion began in 1844. It took thirteen more years for the members of the Philological Society of London to decide that a new comprehensive dictionary of the English language was what the world needed. It would be impossible to imagine a more erudite group of scholars, with specialties ranging from anthropology to zoology, but all masters of linguistics. (J. R. R. Tolkien, an inventor of languages himself, was on one of the later committees.) These men (and regrettably, because of the time, they were all men) were experts in Sanskrit, ancient Hebrew, and Latin, readers of cuneiform and Egyptian hieroglyphs; but above all they were passionately devoted to their own language, English.

The first committee estimated that the project would take no more than ten years to complete and would fill four volumes. In reality, the dictionary was initially completed in 1928, over eighty years after the first proposals were made. Instead of four volumes, it covered forty.

I refer to it being initially completed because the fact is it never was finished and never will be. The editors of what would come to be known as the *Oxford English Dictionary* realized that since language is always growing, changing, and adapting, no dictionary is ever finished.[1] The fact that the greatest linguistic minds of the day could so monumentally underestimate such a task hints at the complexity I mentioned above— not just of the English language, but of language itself.

We can theorize about words and how they work. We can task the greatest minds with listing and outlining and defining them. We can analyze the structures we use to put them into language, but in the end the way words work is an inexpressible mystery. Almost without our awareness they do their thing, lighting up the neural pathways in our brains. We use words to define other words because words are all we have. But ultimately they are only clumsy bricks. Words are, in one sense, beyond words; even the simple ones are often indefinable.

Indefinable words—words that require paragraphs and parables to provide even a hint of all they might possibly mean. *Love* and *hope* are two of the most obvious examples. Of course the *Oxford English Dictionary* lists definitions for them, but they fail miserably because *love* and *hope* are bigger than words. Their meanings cannot be contained by syllables, cannot be fully expressed by the sounds we make with our voices. Groups of letters hint at the inexpressible; they are sounds we put to mysteries. They fascinate and amaze me.

WHY *HESED*?

You have every right to ask yourself how someone could become so obsessed with a single word that they would attempt to write an entire book about it. It's a fair question.

As I try to reconstruct the story of how I became enamored with the word *hesed*, I find that at each step along the way my memory fails me somehow. Some years ago, while working through the laments of the Old Testament, I encountered this remarkable word for the first time. I had studied Hebrew as an undergraduate at Western Kentucky University, but I cannot remember my professors talking about this word. The truth is, they probably did, but I simply wasn't listening.

One of the fascinating features of biblical laments, which so captured my imagination, was the way every one transitions. These psalms begin lamenting (which is still a form of worship), and then at some unpredictable point they transition and begin to praise. This shift usually takes place by means of the Hebrew letter *vav*, which is usually translated "and" or "but." It is as if the lamenter finally exhausts himself and turns back to the God he was complaining to or about. (The sole exception is Psalm 88, which laments all the way to the end.)

In three important laments, Psalms 13 and 69 and Jeremiah's Lamentations, the word *hesed* appears at this turning point. It marks the transition from despair to hope, from emptiness to a new possibility of becoming filled once more. It's as if David and Jeremiah had run out of doubt and despair, had run out of words—except for this one untranslatable word. They could not exhaust its bottomless supply of hope, and by grace it rose to the surface of their lament, transforming it to praise. Their self-centered "I" mercifully became the God-centered "Thou." The pain and frustration and anger were not wiped away but rather transformed by entering the world of this untranslatable, three-letter, two-syllable word, *hesed*. Here are those three transitions:

> But I have trusted in your *hesed*. (Ps 13:5)

> But as for me, LORD,
> my prayer to you is for a time of favor.
> In your abundant *hesed*, God,
> answer me with your sure salvation. (Ps 69:13)

> Because of the LORD's *hesed*
> we do not perish,
> for his mercies never end. (Lam 3:22)

The next step in the process of becoming obsessed with hesed has also been lost to memory, which is hard to understand considering that my life has been so changed by it. As I remember, in the midst of a radio interview with one of my scholarly heroes, I mentioned my newfound fascination with hesed. I distinctly remembered him saying, "Oh, that is the defining characteristic of God." That statement, coming from someone whose scholarship I so admired, lit the fuse. A few years later in a follow-up interview I reminded him of this statement. He insisted he never made it.

The final step involved the discovery of a working definition of this indefinable word. Again, the details have been lost. Looking back through the articles and notes I have collected over the years (two fifteen-hundred-page notebooks full!) I cannot find a trace of it anywhere. I don't think I'm clever enough to have come up with it on my own, and so I do not claim it as my own original definition, though sadly I cannot give a proper attribution. It will provide our initial, ever-incomplete working definition:

> *Hesed:* When the person from whom I have a right to expect nothing gives me everything.

So in the midst of researching a different topic I discovered this remarkable word. (Perhaps it discovered me.) I learned about it in the course of discussions I might not have had and read about it in a source that might not exist. Like the members of the dictionary committee in 1844, I monumentally underestimated the task of writing a book on hesed. What I thought would take a year took ten.

In the course of working on this book I realized that understanding hesed is a lifelong journey. None of us will ever get to the end of it in this life. This book is just the beginning of an exploration, an invitation to join in the journey of the vast world that is the word *hesed*, the greatest sacramental word in the Hebrew Bible.

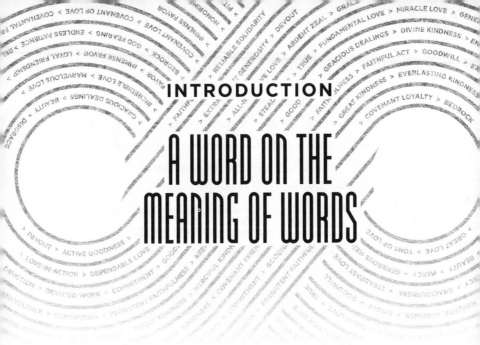

INTRODUCTION

A WORD ON THE MEANING OF WORDS

The Bible puts words to what is beyond words. Because it is God's Word, it perfectly achieves this impossible goal. It invites you and me to a new perspective made possible only by the Spirit *and* the Word, if only we will lovingly *listen* (in Hebrew, *shema*). Before we delve into a detailed examination of some specific passages that contain the word *hesed*, let's take a brief, broad overview of the way words work in general.

Traditionally the first thing readers do when they become interested in a specific word is look up its history or etymology in a dictionary. This is often interesting. For example, the word *panic* traces its origins back to antiquity and the pagan god Pan. If you were to come upon this half-man, half-goat creature in the woods (imagine a scary Mr. Tumnus), you would experience the "panic terror."

In the case of *hesed*, the etymology is interesting but ultimately misleading. Studying *hesed* reveals the frustrating side of word histories. Some dictionaries simply state that its etymology is uncertain. Others claim that *hesed* is derived from *hasida* (stork). "The stork," they say, "is known as the pious bird." (In contrast to the ostrich, which is used in the Bible to portray foolishness as the worst mother in the animal kingdom. See Job 39:13-18.) But an examination of the primary sources fails to reveal anything useful about storks that might help us understand *hesed*. Storks are not mentioned in the Mishnah, and a digital search of the Talmud does not show a single occurrence. In Leviticus 11:19 and Deuteronomy 14:18 storks are listed, along with bats, as unclean. So the dictionaries, with their etymologies of pious birds, don't come close to revealing the significance of *hesed*. One wonders whether this etymology was reverse engineered.

Scholars have realized that, though they may sometimes be helpful, an overreliance on word backgrounds or etymology can often lead to significant misunderstanding. Language is too complex and fluid. Words shift in meaning over time. This is referred to as "diachronic" meaning (through time). There are other, more reliable ways to determine the meaning of a given word in a biblical text.

The context in which a word appears is a more reliable way to determine its meaning. If I shout, "It's a bomb!" at a football game, you expect to see a long forward pass. But if I shout the same words in a crowded airport, you should expect a panic. The context determines the meaning. What does the word *key* mean? If I'm standing in front of a locked door, you assume I mean the piece of metal used to unlock the door. If I'm sitting at a piano, you know I'm talking about the key of a song. At a lecture, *key* probably refers to the central idea of a concept. The context allows us to understand the specific meaning of the word at a particular time. (We don't even know how to pronounce some words apart from their context. How do you pronounce *lead* or *bow*?) This context-derived meaning is known as "synchronic" meaning, the meaning at one specific point in time.

In the pages that follow we will listen to the word *hesed* in its immediate context in a number of passages and try to understand just what the meaning was for the author at that particular point in time. This will give us the best preliminary introduction to the world of hesed.

A BROAD OVERVIEW

Let's begin with a broad overview of our word. It's composed of three Hebrew consonants, khet (ח), samek (ס), and dalet (ד), read from right to left. Its first syllable is pronounced with a hard guttural *h*. It looks like this in Hebrew: חסד. Unlike most Hebrew words, which place the stress on the final syllable, when *hesed* is pronounced the stress is on the first syllable.[1]

It is tempting to say *hesed* is the most important word in the Hebrew Scriptures. One Bible encyclopedia calls it one of the most important theological words in the Old Testament; another lexicon describes it as the most sacramental word in the Bible. A good case can be made for the claim that it has the largest range of meaning of any word in the Hebrew language, and perhaps in any language.

Hesed occurs nearly 250 times in the Hebrew Bible throughout all of the three major divisions—the Law, the Prophets, and the Writings. The majority of occurrences (127) are in the Psalms.

In a very broad, general sense, *hesed*'s meaning, as happens with many words, subtly shifts between chronologically earlier and later Bible passages. This does not override the meaning it has at any one specific moment (synchronic meaning), however. If we try to make the case that *hesed* somehow progressively developed over time, the evidence is against us. So the following examples are only generalities to help us get started.

In Genesis *hesed* indicates an exceptional favor from God, something that has not been earned but graciously given. For example, the first time the word appears in the Hebrew Bible (Gen 19:19), Lot is asking God whether he can flee to Zoar instead of to the mountains. He has no right to expect that God will grant this indulgence but in his desperation he asks, and God in his kindness allows it. In Exodus, where the word occurs only four times, it leaps ahead in meaning and is used by God himself to describe his character. This demonstrates the fact that word meaning is not a simple matter of growth over time.

In the vast majority of references in the historical books, *hesed* has to do with a reciprocal expectation between two human beings, most often in stories about David. The expectation is not, strictly speaking, part of a written covenant but rather an aspect of relationship, though covenants come from hesed. In Psalms *hesed* is celebrated in song and often magnified by several choice words that appear in close proximity to it. In Proverbs *hesed* is mentioned primarily as something lacking in humans, though in Proverbs 14:34 and 25:9-10 it is curiously translated "disgrace."[2] In the Prophets, where the word occurs only twenty-eight times, the abundant hesed of God is in sharp contrast with the fragile hesed of men and women, which disappears like the morning dew. But ultimately it is God's lovingkindness that is the source of the new covenant with Israel and Judah.

The vast range of *hesed* is also made evident by the staggering number of English words translators employ in a frustrated effort to render it (see appendix B). The King James Version uses fourteen different words. It even borrows an elegant new word from Miles Coverdale's 1535 translation: "loving-kindness." Coverdale made up this beautiful word specifically in an attempt to translate *hesed*, and it remains the favorite choice of many. But all these words barely began to capture the semantic range of *hesed*. Later translations resort to all kinds of compound terms, which provide a clue to the difficulty of reducing the Hebrew *hesed* to a single English word.

LINGUISTIC GRAVITY

To borrow a concept from the world of physics, we might say that *hesed* is a word with an enormous mass. The greater the size of the object, the greater the gravitational pull it exerts. Earth revolves around the Sun because its great mass pulls us toward it. (The centripetal force, which pulls our planet away from the Sun, is perfectly balanced to keep us in a steady orbit.) One of the fascinating features of *hesed* is its tendency to draw other words to itself by means of its "linguistic gravity." It's as if in struggling to express the inexpressible, the original writer was forced to enlist other words beside *hesed* to help convey its meaning. Sometimes the additional word is joined with the letter *vav*, usually translated "and"; hence, for example, "hesed and truth" (the most prevalent combination). In other examples the additional word occurs in close proximity, usually in what is referred to as poetic parallelism.

There are eight principal words that *hesed* draws to itself in this way:

- truth, *emet* (אמת) (Gen 24:27, 49; 32:10; 47:29; Ex 34:6; Josh 2:14; 2 Sam 2:6; 15:20; Ps 25:10; 40:10; 57:3; 61:7; 69:13; 85:10; 86:15; 89:14; Prov 3:3; 14:22; 16:6; 20:28; Hos 4:1)

- mercy/compassion, *raham* (רחם) (Ps 25:6; 103:4; Jer 16:5; Dan 1:9; Hos 2:19; Zech 7:9)

- covenant, *berith* (ברית) (Deut 7:9, 12; 1 Kings 8:23; 2 Chron 6:14; Neh 1:5; Dan 9:4)

- justice, *mishpat* (משפט) (Ps 100:5; Jer 9:24; Hos 12:6)

- faithfulness, *amuna* (אמונה) (Ps 89:24; 98:3)

- goodness, *tov* (טוב) (Ps 23:6; 86:5)

- favor, *hen* (חן) (Esther 2:17)

- righteousness, *tsadik* (צדק) (Prov 21:21)

In Genesis 24:27 Abraham's servant praises God for not forsaking his *hesed and* his truth. In Jeremiah 16:5 the prophet, speaking for God, declares that he has removed his peace from the people, as well as his *hesed and* his compassion. In Deuteronomy 7:9 Moses proclaims, "The LORD your God is God, the faithful God who keeps his covenant *and hesed* for a thousand generations with those who love him." Hosea, in presenting God's case against Jacob's heirs, says in Hosea 12:6, "You must return to your God. / Maintain *hesed and* justice." Ethan, in Psalm 89:24, records the Lord promising his "faithfulness *and hesed*" to David, who we will see was a frequent focus of God's *hesed*. David himself sings in Psalm 23:6, "Only goodness *and hesed* will pursue me / all the days of my life." In the book of Esther we are told that Esther "obtained favor *and hesed* in his [the king's] sight more than all the virgins" (Esther 2:17 ASV). And finally, Solomon in Proverbs 21:21 promises life and righteousness to anyone who pursues righteousness *and hesed*.

Hesed attracts words to itself in another way as scholars, attempting to translate it, are forced to use multiple English words. A single word is rarely enough in a given context to express all that *hesed* means, so translators are forced to pile on adjectives. When you are reading an English translation of the Hebrew Bible this is a good way to determine whether the word you're looking at is *hesed*. In modern translations it is rarely rendered simply as "loyalty," but as "covenant loyalty" or "unswerving loyalty." It is not just "love" but "merciful" or "loyal" or "relentless" or "enduring" or "extravagant" love. The list goes on and on (see the list at the beginning of this book). The meaning draws other words in an attempt to express the inexpressible. In the end, hesed is as much a world as a word. These other gravitational words help to define its boundaries and estimate the remarkable mass of its meaning.

It's important as we move forward to remember that the purpose of this journey is not to become preoccupied with a single word. Let's let go of the illusion that *hesed* can be reduced to one English "literal" word and instead see it as a key that can open a door into an entire world—the world of God's own heart, the world of loving our neighbor and perhaps even our enemies. As we begin, let's ask for strength to bring everything to bear in this process of loving God by listening to his Word—all our hearts, our souls, and everything that we are (see Deut 6:5). Let's ask for the grace to be in awe of the God who, when he opened the door of his life to us, had this word consistently on his lips, remembering that even though we have no right to expect anything from him he is pleased to give us everything. He is pleased to open his heart and life to us precisely because he is the God of hesed.

So this is the word *hesed*. Two syllables we speak with our teeth and tongue, a word we put to the mystery of a God who gives us not simply a second chance but more chances than we can possibly imagine (see Mt 18:21-22). It provides a reason for hope, our only real reason for hope. Though we will never exhaustively define *hesed*, we can nonetheless begin the journey toward understanding it. We can listen to it in the pages of the Hebrew Bible. We can see how it was lived out in the lives of people like Moses, David, and Ruth, how they became the objects of God's hesed, and ultimately how it became incarnate in Jesus of Nazareth. It is an infinite but, paradoxically, not an endless journey, for we believe and hope and trust there will be a final destination.

PART ONE

THE GOD OF HESED

1

OPENING THE DOOR

"I want to tell you about the night I killed Ted Morris."

Tommy Pigage opened his court-mandated appearance at the Trigg County High School MADD meeting with those trembling words. Standing in the back of the gym was Elizabeth Morris, Ted's grieving mother. In time she would find it in herself not simply to forgive but to unofficially adopt the young man who had collided with her son while driving drunk. Her husband, Frank, a part-time preacher and a driver for UPS, would baptize Tommy with his own hands. Years later, Tommy still called his new parents every day between 4 and 5 p.m. Though Tommy had no right to expect anything from them, Ted's parents opened the door of their life to Tommy. In the process, everything changed.[1]

Samuel Sesay is the director of Edunations, a ministry that builds schools in remote villages in Sierra Leone, West Africa. When in 2014 Ebola broke out in the region, the ministry shifted from building schools to serving those who were suffering from the disease by providing food for families during the forced three-week quarantine. There were rumors of children dying not from the disease but from the isolation period, when many parents could not provide food.

Earlier, one of the ministry workers, John, had to be removed from his position after serious charges of misappropriation were proven to be true. Samuel had to enforce the decision and tell John he could no longer work with Edunations. John's response was to hire a local witch doctor to pronounce a death curse on Samuel.

Later, in the midst of the plague, a woman who lived in John's house inadvertently played with a child whose mother had just died from Ebola. John's entire household of twenty-three people was immediately placed under a three-week forced quarantine. A family that large would not survive without outside help, which by this point the government was no longer able to provide.

When he heard the news, Samuel made providing food for John's family a priority for the ministry. When John saw one of the workers delivering care packages, he was so overcome that he nearly broke through the rope demarcating his quarantined house. His family was sustained, and thankfully no one else contracted Ebola. John wept publically and asked the church to pray for him. Samuel's openness to care for the person who had desired his death opened a door in John's life that would have otherwise remained forever closed.

In Ann Arbor, Michigan, in 1996 eighteen-year-old Keshia Thomas showed up to protest a rally of the white supremacist group known as the KKK. Keshia and her friends were in a separate fenced-off space when one of the KKK members inadvertently wandered into her group. Someone shouted, "There's a Klansman!" and the protesters began to retaliate.

Then Keshia threw herself into the fray, placing her own body between the Klansman and the outraged protestors, possibly saving the man's life in the process. At that moment someone took a picture that became the *Time/Life* photo of the year. Keshia's radical act of courage gave birth to a movement that has inspired thousands more to consider opening the door of their lives in forgiveness and reconciliation.[2]

Forgiving the murderer of your only son, feeding someone who has placed a curse on you, offering yourself to save a man who has dedicated his life to persecuting and destroying yours. We hear these kinds of sacrificial, heroic, impossibly forgiving stories and wonder how someone could open the door of their life to another in such an inexpressible way. We are wordless before these kinds of stories because they press the boundaries of language to express. There is no word that communicates the miracle of someone opening their life to someone who has no right to expect anything from them. Or is there?

The Bible reveals the God of hesed, who has opened the door of his life to you and me. Though we are responsible for the death of his only Son and have, in effect, cursed him, he covered us with his body, his blood, and saved us long before we might have accepted him. We have no right to expect anything from him, the Holy One. Yet he has extended himself to us, has invited us to enter his world, has made our story a part of his story, has opened his life to the inevitable possibility of being hurt, disappointed, and wounded by you and me.

The story is repeated again and again in Scripture. God invites Adam and Eve into his life, only to be wounded by their willingness to believe Satan over him. He extends himself to the Israelites, to Moses, and to David, only to be rejected, to be hurt by their stubborn disbelief. "How long will these people despise me?" God whispers to Moses in Numbers 14:11. "What fault did your fathers find in me?" he laments in Jeremiah 2:5. Ultimately, in Jesus of Nazareth he extends himself, personally and intimately, calls us friends, is vulnerable, only to be wounded, abandoned, and crucified, when at any moment he might have disappeared over the hill into the vast hiding place of the

Judean desert. Though we had no right to expect anything from him, he freely gave us everything.

At the heart of this relentless and extravagant act of God himself, central to the indescribable mystery of the opening of the door of his life, is the Hebrew word *hesed*. When God definitively reveals himself to Moses, the word is twice upon his lips. When he reaches out to David, it is the word on which their relationship and David's throne rest. The psalmists sing about it. The prophets lament its fragileness in us. And God himself hopes that our response to his hesed will be an infinitely smaller, yet still indescribable, expression of our own hesed. Jesus will expand on it in his parables and incarnate it in his own life.

This small three-letter word, חסד, seems to always be there when the door is open from one life to another, when the unexpected and undeserved gift of one's life is offered with no strings attached, when inexpressible acts of adoption, forgiveness, and courage occur that leave us speechless.

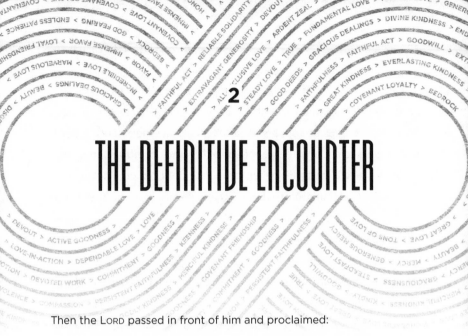

2

THE DEFINITIVE ENCOUNTER

Then the LORD passed in front of him and proclaimed:

Yahweh—Yahweh is a compassionate and gracious God, slow to anger and rich in *hesed* and truth, maintaining *hesed* to a thousand generations, forgiving wrongdoing, rebellion, and sin. But He will not leave the guilty unpunished, bringing the consequences of the fathers' wrongdoing on the children and grandchildren to the third and fourth generation.

EXODUS 34:6-7 HCSB

The image of the fragments of the first set of tablets, broken by Moses in frustration and anger, lying along the trail on one of the lower slopes of Mount Sinai, has become a preoccupation for me. Those wondrous tablets referred to as the "testimony" (*edut*) (Ex 32:15), covered with the handwriting of God himself, were discarded in the sand. Perhaps they are up there still, covered in the dust of millennia.

Moses lies shattered too, broken before the Lord. The fragile dream he fought to keep alive, of God himself leading the people into the Land of Promise, had fallen to pieces when he heard those devastating words, "I will not go up with you" (Ex 33:3).

Later, in the tent of meeting where he meets face to face with the Lord, Moses asks God to teach him his ways (Ex 33:13). If you read between the lines, it appears Moses is still concerned that the Lord might not accompany the people into the land. It will be a nagging suspicion he will carry, along with two new stone tablets, back up the mountain. God had promised that his angel would go with them. But the Lord, tragically for Moses, would not go, lest he destroy the "stiff-necked people" along the way.

Moses, at over eighty years old (Ex 7:7), has gone up and down steep Sinai at least nine times by this point. He has experienced the plagues in Egypt and the endless complaining of the people. He has offered his very life to save them. In the intimacy of the tent of meeting the Lord at last gives in to Moses' plea: "My presence will go with you, and I will give you rest" (Ex 33:14). Moses has found favor (*hen*), one of those words *hesed* draws to itself. In response he impetuously blurts out, "Please, let me see your glory!"

The response of God is not what anyone would have expected. The One who spoke the universe into existence and parted the Red Sea, who was accompanied by terrifying lightning, thunder, and deep darkness, speaks of tenderly placing Moses in the cleft of a rock and gently covering him with the same hand that shaped the galaxies. He will cause all of his "goodness," which is his glory, to pass before Moses. At the right moment he will take the protective hand away after he has passed by and allow Moses to see his back (Ex 33:19-23).

IN THE MORNING

Early the next morning, Moses obediently carves out two blank replacement tablets and makes his way, all alone, up the mountain once more. This will be his last trip up Sinai. For the time being he will be done with mountaintops. What is about to happen on Sinai will change everything—forever.

The cloud of the presence descends, enveloping Moses. God will reveal the deepest part of himself to Moses, his friend, who is standing alone beside the Lord. This is the moment of ultimate revelation, the definitive encounter. Compared to Exodus 34, God's meeting with Abraham at the binding of Isaac is just a prelude (see Gen 22). Here, God is about to reveal to Moses, and to us, who he essentially is! The undefinable is about to define himself.

For the only time in Scripture, the Lord repeats his personal, unspeakable name twice (Ex 34:6). Out of respect it should be translated "the LORD." Moses would have recognized this name from when he first heard it, beside the burning bush (Ex 3:14). A possible translation is "I am who I am" or "I will be who I will be." It is a name that expresses not simply the fact that God is a being, but that he is Being itself. Some within Judaism claim that this is not actually the personal name of God but rather a definition of what that unspeakable name means.

What follows is a list of the personal attributes of the One who is Being itself. In Judaism they are called the Shelosh-Esreh Middot Ha Rakhamim, the Thirteen Attributes of Mercy.[1]

The order is significant. Notice that the first defining word is not holiness or power but compassion. The word in Hebrew is *racham*, which can be translated "compassion," "tender mercy," or "pity." It is linked to the word *rechem* or "womb" and connotes the love elicited by a helpless baby from a mother or father (see Ps 103:13; Jer 21:7). Though he has yet to reveal himself as Father, the first word used by God to describe his character is a parental word. It is another one of the words that *hesed* frequently draws to itself.

The next word the Lord uses to define himself is *hen*, which can be translated "grace" or "favor." It appears in the commonly used biblical phrase "find favor in the eyes of." Both Noah and Moses were said to have found *hen* or favor in God's sight (Gen 6:8; Ex 33:12).

Next comes the phrase "slow to anger," or "slow of anger." This attribute of God has already been demonstrated multiple times, beginning with Adam and Eve in the garden and up to the golden calf incident. To those who are fond of speaking of the "angry Old Testament God," here, as God describes himself, he asserts that he is slow to become angry. This is woven intimately into the first two traits. A compassionate and gracious person never angers easily. Later we will see that this statement becomes the basis for a musical theme that will be repeated throughout the Hebrew Bible.

The next term the Lord speaks is based on a word that appears more often than any other in association with *hesed*: *emet* (fifty-one times). It can be translated "true," "reliable," "dependable," or "trustworthy." The Gospel of John's "grace and truth" (Jn 1:14) is a precise echo of the Hebrew *hesed vemet*.

Next God speaks of forgiving wrongdoing, rebellion, and sin. The word used for forgiving (*nasa*) means to carry or to lift. Essentially God is taking the load of the wrongdoing, rebellion, and sin upon himself, which is involved whenever forgiveness is extended to another person. In a sense, when we forgive someone, we are carrying the load by taking away the burden of guilt from them. The following three words express the full range of sin. The first, *avon*, has to do with guilt. The second, *pesha*, has to do with breaking away or becoming a rebel, hence "rebellion." The final term, *hata*, is the most common word for sin, appearing 580 times in the Hebrew Bible. It connotes "missing the mark." The burden of the full range of all of these aspects of disobedience and rebellion God says he will carry or lift as an essential part of his character.

If we had only the first half of this self-revelation of the character of God, we might be tempted to see him as someone we could perpetually take advantage of (see Rom 6:1), but in the final attribute God describes himself as the one who will not leave the guilty unpunished. We will see that justice and hesed also sometimes appear together. The apparent tension between perfect hesed and perfect justice is sustained throughout the Hebrew Bible. Here, as God lays out his defining characteristics as compassion, grace, mercy, forgiveness, kindness, and love to a thousand generations, he makes clear that wrongdoing will eventually be cleansed.

One misunderstanding needs to be cleared up here. When God speaks of the consequences of the sins of the fathers being brought to the children and grandchildren, this does not mean, as many translations reflect, that the later generations will be punished or forced to pay for their fathers' and grandfathers' sins. Deuteronomy 24:16 makes it clear: "Fathers are not to be put to death for their children, and children are not to be put to death for their fathers; each person will be put to death for his own sin." As does Ezekiel 18:1-4, 20:

> The word of the LORD came to me: "What do you mean by using this proverb concerning the land of Israel:
>
> 'The fathers eat sour grapes,
>   and the children's teeth are set on edge'?
>
> As I live"—this is the declaration of the Lord GOD—"you will no longer use this proverb in Israel. Look, every life belongs to me. The life of the father is like the life of the son—both belong to me. The person who sins is the one who will die. . . .
>
> The person who sins is the one who will die. A son won't suffer punishment for the father's iniquity, and a father won't suffer punishment for the son's iniquity. The righteousness of the righteous person will be on him, and the wickedness of the wicked person will be on him.

So in this definitive encounter God reveals his infinite compassion and mercy as well as his perfect justice. His fundamental character is grace and truth and, accordingly, he will definitively deal with the problem of sin. Now, what about the two occurrences of our word *hesed* in this passage?

The fact that the word is used twice is the first indication that this is a key attribute. In verse 6 God is said to be rich or abundant (*rav*) in *hesed*. Verse 7 says that he maintains (*natzar*) *hesed*. This word is used of someone guarding a vineyard or keeping watch over the tongue. God is faithfully maintaining or keeping a guard over his hesed.

A NEW UNDERSTANDING

When Moses limped up the mountain he might have expected smoke, fire, and thunder. He certainly hoped for the two new stone tablets to be re-inscribed. But upon hearing that God is full of hesed he realizes that though he has a right to expect nothing, everything will be freely given to him. When Moses hears that this abundant source of mercy, kindness, and love is also maintained and watched over by the One who is at that very moment protecting him with his hand, a seismic shift occurs in his understanding of God. The One who spoke the universe into being, who molded planets and moons with his hand, is now using that same hand to tenderly cover his fragile friend. From this moment Moses' relationship with God undergoes a change that will forever revolutionize everything for Israel—and for us.

In response to what he has heard, Moses bows down in worship. At the burning bush Moses had taken off his shoes in obedience to God, in recognition of the fact that he was standing on holy ground. But there is no word of his responding to God in worship there. In Exodus 4:31 the people, including Moses, worshiped upon first hearing of their deliverance. But this moment feels fundamentally different. Moses is celebrating the worth ("worth-shiping") of the God who has just revealed himself while protecting Moses with his hand. The God who is slow to anger and compassionate yet at the same time perfectly just, this God of hesed, has opened the door of his life to Moses.

Compare the levels of intimacy in Exodus 19:25, where Moses stood with the quaking people at the bottom of the mountain, and this moment. Now Moses is alone with the Lord. The God of the universe has spoken the definitive words that perfectly describe his character to the person who will henceforth be known as God's friend. Moses has asked to see God's glory. The Lord has responded by revealing the true nature of that glory: compassion, mercy, truth, kindness, hesed. Moses now knows the Lord as no one has yet known him, even Abraham. The depth of his new knowledge is revealed in the request he makes as he worships the God he now knows is a God of lovingkindness.

The first words from Moses' lips reveal his new understanding of God as well as his heart for the people. "Please, go with us," he stammers. That sliver of doubt that God still might not go with his people into the land has been weighing on Moses' heart. He acknowledges the stubbornness of the people, and so in his request that God accompany them, Moses is asking for something he admits he and they do not deserve. The request is based on the new revelation of hesed.

When the person from whom I have a right to expect nothing gives me everything.

The broken prophet, kneeling before the Lord in worship, is asking for *hesed because now he knows he can.* The finger of God will freshly inscribe the blank tablets he brought with him. The One who is slow to anger will eventually accompany the wayward people into the land after their initial infuriating refusal to enter, just as he was with them in the wilderness.

Moses makes his way back down the trail, past the broken shards of the first two tablets. His face is fearfully radiant. Jonathan Sacks notes that when Moses descended from the mountain the first time, his face was not shining.[2] Only now, having seen and heard the character of the hesed of God, is his face aglow.

A freshly repentant people wait for Moses at the bottom of the mountain. In time they will set out for the Promised Land, led by the promised pillar of the cloud of God's presence. They will complain about the hardships, about the lack of water and food, but the God of hesed, who is slow to anger, will provide protection and living water and manna. When they arrive at the border of the land they will fearfully refuse to enter, and Moses will be forced to remind God of the words he had spoken on the mountain (Num 14:17-25). True to his word, the second and third generation will suffer the consequences of their parents' sin of disbelief in the wilderness, but after a generation's time (forty years) they will enter the land.

Those original tablets, the first "testimony" that now lies shattered along the trail up Sinai, the remarkable shards covered with the handwriting of God himself, Moses had apparently passed right by on his way back to meet with God. What would the inestimable value be of even a fragment, perhaps a corner with a single letter? And yet, how much infinitely more precious are these words we have, the self-revelation of God, opening the door of his life to Moses and Israel and you and me. Telling us who he is at the very depth of his being, he who is Being itself.

It seems that we humans can relate to only one half of this revelation at a time. Either we imagine ourselves before an all-gracious God who indulges any imaginable behavior, or we find ourselves standing in front of an eternally angry, punishing God who is impossible to please no matter how spotless our behavior. It's almost as if our imaginations cannot embrace a God who is perfectly loving and perfectly just at the same time. But that is the God whose hand is covering Moses as these words are spoken. He shows his loving-kindness to thousands and yet is perfect in his justice by refusing to erase the consequences of sin.

How do you relate to a God who reveals himself in this way? What should be our posture before him? Why not begin with the posture Moses assumed there on top of the holy mountain. What other possible attitude could we take except to fall on our knees and worship this Complete One, whose love is seamless and whose justice is perfect?

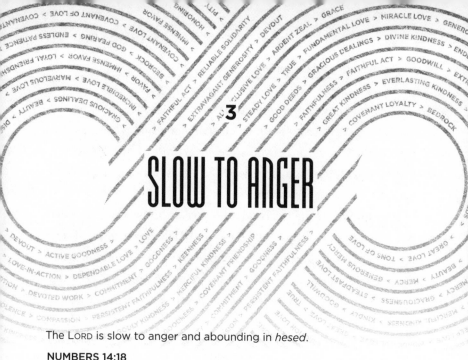

3

SLOW TO ANGER

The LORD is slow to anger and abounding in *hesed*.

NUMBERS 14:18

It has been roughly a year since Moses was on his knees, worshiping the God of *hesed*. It has been a time of struggle, of complaining, of betrayal and grinding frustration. And now, finally, the people have arrived on the border of the Promised Land.

In obedience to God's command, twelve representatives of the tribes are sent to reconnoiter the land. They discover conditions there just as promising as God had promised. It is indeed a land flowing with milk and honey. They cut a cluster of grapes to take back—a single cluster so massive it took two men to lug it on a pole (Num 13:23). They show the people the evidence they've gathered, the grapes as well as some pomegranates and figs. After their time in the wilderness this evidence must have been mouthwatering. The gift of the land was an act of *hesed* in and of itself. The grumbling people had no right to expect anything from the Lord, yet here he provides everything and more.

But then it all goes sideways. Ten of the spies report that the people who inhabit the land are strong and live in walled cities. This is a bad sign since it hints that taking the land may involve besieging the larger fortified towns.

One spy, Caleb, interrupts in verse 30: "We can do this!" he says. "We must do this." The ten respond with more fear, more disbelief. Perhaps they are exaggerating (perhaps not) when they whine, "We even saw the Nephilim there!" (Num 13:33; see Gen 6:4). And that is all it takes.

In Numbers 14:1 the people give in to all their worst fears, crying all night. Everything rapidly disintegrates. They want to go back to Egypt. They decide to appoint another leader who will take up the task of guiding them back into the wilderness, back to Egypt and the world they know—slavery. Upon hearing this Moses and his brother, Aaron, fall facedown before the assembly, while Joshua and Caleb entreat the people to trust that the Lord will be true to his promise. He will empower them to take the land. Their discourse is summed up with the statement, "The Lord is with us!" The response of the people? They threatened to stone the two fearless and faithful young men.

Just then the glory of God appears at the tent of meeting, a sign for Moses to go and speak with the Lord. Inside the intimacy of the tent, where they meet face to face, the Lord unburdens himself to his friend, Moses. They truly are intimates, drawn together by their mutual frustration with the unbelief and complaining of the people.

"How long will these people despise me?" God says (Num 14:11). To "despise" or "abandon" (*na'ats*) the Lord is a sin that reveals the nature of all sin. It cannot go unpunished because by abandoning God we reject him and willfully place ourselves outside his hesed (see Deut 31:20). In one sense this sin is unpardonable because the people who despise the Lord also despise his mercy, the very source of his forgiveness, thus rendering themselves unpardonable. The Lord concludes, "Let's start all over again." He will wipe the people out with a plague and begin again with Moses (a strategy to which he had already resorted with Noah and the flood; Gen 6–8).

Moses' defense and intercession for the people stand on two legs. First, God should not destroy the people because it will destroy his "fame" with the Egyptians, who have witnessed the deliverance of the people of God. Second, and more to the point, it would violate the character that God had revealed on the mountain. Had he not said he was slow to anger and abundant in hesed? In a remarkable passage, Moses word for word reminds God of what he had said a year ago on the sacred mountain.

"Just as you have spoken," Moses says as he proceeds to remind the Lord that he is abounding in hesed. He concludes by begging for the forgiveness the people do not deserve, "in keeping with the greatness of your *hesed*" (Num 14:17-19). Just after the revelation on the mountaintop, Moses had asked for something he knew he did not deserve: for God to change his mind and accompany the people through the wilderness to the Promised Land. Now, once again, Moses asks for forgiveness *according to hesed*, simply because he now knows he has the freedom to ask for what he and the people do not deserve. This new boldness is born from the initial and groundbreaking revelation of Exodus 34. It can be confidently requested because of the revealed identity of the Lord, who is slow to anger and rich in hesed. Because hesed is a part of the Lord's identity, it becomes the basis of the hope of the people who are known by his name.

If ever the Lord will ultimately demonstrate by his actions that he is indeed slow to anger, it will be now. At the very moment the people are about to receive the fulfillment of the promise by entering the land, they "despise" the Lord and Moses his spokesman. But Moses' plea is based on the knowledge he has of the character of God as it was revealed to him on the mountain. The nation will be preserved precisely because of the richness of God's hesed. The people will not be destroyed as a nation, and in time they will indeed occupy the Land of Promise. Because of Moses' understanding of the hesed of God, he is justified in assuming the Lord will be "more faithful then he has a right to expect."[1]

But there is a problem. If God is truly a God of hesed, why are the people sent back into the wilderness for forty years to eventually die? Why not simply forgive and forget and proceed into the land? This is where the passage helps us see the nature of sin and its inescapable consequences.

The God of hesed has done everything and more to bring the people to the Promised Land. Poised on the border, they refuse to believe—that is, willfully disbelieve—God's promise and speak of their desire to die in the desert (Num 14:2). Disbelief and stubborn refusal to obey and move into the land leave only one possibility: return to the wilderness. And ultimately returning to the wilderness means death—not death to the nation, for God will keep his promise, but to those who despised him. The consequences of the parents' sin will be experienced by the children and their children, meaning all who are alive at the time (Ex 34:7; Num 14:18). But the children and grandchildren will eventually enter the land. They will suffer the effects because that is the nature of sin, but ultimately they will enter the land because of God's hesed, revealed to Moses on the mountain. Had God not said that he would visit the consequences of the fathers' sins on the children? Stubborn disbelief has its own inescapable results.

Yet even in this, God is demonstrating his kindness. To erase the effects of sin would be devastating to the following generations.

Indeed, sin would multiply. But the children and grandchildren will suffer the wilderness consequences of their parents' sin and so eventually enter the Promised Land a changed people.

This generation who despised God provides the perfect parable for one of C. S. Lewis's explanations of the nature of sin: "There are only two kinds of people in the end: those who say to God, 'Thy will be done,' and those to whom God says, in the end, 'Thy will be done.' All that are in Hell, choose it. Without that self-choice there could be no Hell."[2]

In this story, God's will was clearly the provision of a land flowing with milk and honey. The people's will was that another leader, not chosen by God, return them to slavery in Egypt and death in the wilderness. On the verge of the Promised Land, God in effect said, "Very well, your will be done." So the people returned to the wilderness as they willed, for another forty years. Still, because of the riches of God's hesed, their children and grandchildren eventually would enter and possess the land.

The opening phrase of Moses' reminder to the Lord, "The Lord is slow to anger and rich in *hesed*," would become a formula in the subsequent centuries. It is sung by David in three of his psalms:

But you, LORD, are a compassionate and gracious God,
slow to anger and abounding in *hesed* and truth. (Ps 86:15)

He revealed his ways to Moses,
his deeds to the people of Israel.
The LORD is compassionate and gracious,
slow to anger and abounding in *hesed*.
He will not always accuse us
or be angry forever.
He has not dealt with us as our sins deserve
or repaid us according to our iniquities. (Ps 103:7-10)

The LORD is gracious and compassionate,

slow to anger and great in *hesed*.

The LORD is good to everyone;

his compassion rests on all he has made. (Ps 145:8-9)

It is remembered by Nehemiah as the people lament for their sin as a nation but still hope in the God of *hesed*:

They refused to listen

and did not remember your wonders

you performed among them.

They became stiff-necked and appointed a leader

to return to their slavery in Egypt.

But you are a forgiving God,

gracious and compassionate,

slow to anger and abounding in *hesed*,

and you did not abandon them. (Neh 9:17)

Joel repeats the formula as he calls the people to fresh repentance:

Tear your hearts,

not just your clothes,

and return to the LORD your God.

For he is gracious and compassionate,

slow to anger, abounding in *hesed*,

and he relents from sending disaster. (Joel 2:13; see also Ps 51:1)

Isaiah, looking forward to the future restoration of Israel, spoke for the One who is slow to anger when he said,

"I deserted you for a brief moment,

but I will take you back with abundant compassion [*rachem*].

In a surge of anger

I hid my face from you for a moment,
but I will have compassion on you
with *hesed*,"
says the LORD your Redeemer. (Is 54:7-8)

The God who revealed himself to Moses in Exodus 34 is slow to anger precisely because he is rich in hesed. Though the people continue to break the covenants he makes with them, he keeps keeping them because he is rich in hesed. It is what makes him unlike any other god. He demonstrates his incomparable strength by means of his infinite kindness.

It's difficult for us to imagine how a being who is infinite in power submerses that power in kindness. But a deep realization of this aspect of God's hesed is as revolutionary for us today as it was for Israel more than three thousand years ago. It dismantles that nagging image of the "angry God of the Old Testament." That perception simply has no place in a biblical understanding of who God is.

To be clear, nowhere in Scripture does it say God does not get angry. But that anger does not characterize who he is. It is difficult for us to conceive of an anger that does not lead to sin, but even Paul said, "Be angry and do not sin" (Eph 4:26).

We need to establish in our own minds, for our own sakes, what the implications are of being in relationship with the God who is slow to anger but rich in hesed. He is not an emotionless, passionless deity far off and remote. In his intimacy with and caring for his creatures, anger is as inevitable today as it was in the wilderness. But the Word says he is slow to become angry because he is rich in hesed.

LIKE NO OTHER GOD

Lord God of Israel,
there is no God like you
in heaven or on earth,
who keeps his covenant *and hesed*
with your servants who walk before you
with all their heart.

2 CHRONICLES 6:14 (ALSO 1 KINGS 8:23)

This remarkable moment lies buried in a book we rarely read. But an unbroken line of the hesed of the God of Exodus 34 has brought Solomon to this place. The One who clothed the disobedient Adam and Eve is the One who set his people free and led them in lovingkindness through the wilderness to the glowing land they then refused to enter. He is the God who showered his life-giving, life-preserving hesed on the second and third generations after the first generation who despised him, just as he had promised Moses on the mountain. He is the One who established the throne of Solomon's father, David, on hesed (1 Kings 3:6) despite the king's adultery and lies and murder. And now, here stands David's son, Solomon (or Jedidiah, the name God knows him by).

David has been "gathered to his fathers," but Solomon's mother, Bathsheba, is here to see this. She is weary yet still regal. Solomon has inherited his father's poetic imagination. His lengthy prayer and blessing to dedicate the gleaming new temple is entirely poetic, perhaps even lyrical, though there is no word of any music accompanying it. Perhaps he is chanting the prayer, clothed with "royal majesty" (see 1 Chron 29:25).

Just three chapters after this account in 1 Kings we are told that Solomon will build more temples, but this time for his pagan wives, to the gods Ashtoreth, Chemosh, and Milcom (1 Kings 11). He will soon be overwhelmed by his enemies and will die, a sad and spent force, after forty years on the throne. But for now, in this luminous moment Solomon is the unquestioned king, David's son, dedicating the temple he was chosen over his father to erect.

In 2 Chronicles 5:13 the people sing, "For he is good; his *hesed* endures forever." As a result a cloud that is identified as the glory of the Lord fills the new temple structure. After this, Solomon steps to the front of the awestruck crowd and begins to rhapsodize in poetic prayer.

His opening statement exults in the fact that the Lord who was said to dwell only in darkness has been provided a golden temple, a place to dwell forever (2 Chron 6:1). Then his poem prayer, which fills the entire chapter, begins pouring out blessings on the Lord who spoke to his father, David, and fulfilled each and every one of his promises.

Solomon stands on an enormous bronze platform, kneels, and with outstretched arms picks up the song that Israel had sung five hundred years before when they crossed the Red Sea on dry land, a song that celebrated the hesed of the God who saved his people (Ex 15:11-13). Surely there was no God like theirs. Moses picked up the refrain in Deuteronomy 3:23-25, pleading with God to allow him to enter the land he had so longed to see. The basis of his plea was the same as

Solomon's statement: "There is no God like you . . . who keeps his covenant of *hesed*" (2 Chron 6:14).

The rest of Solomon's long prayer focuses on every eventuality of the provision of the unique covenant of hesed given by the One who was about to inhabit his golden temple. The covenant will be in effect when individuals sin against their neighbors, when the people are defeated because of their sin, when there is drought due also to sin, or when there is famine or pestilence or blight or an attack by their many enemies. The hesed that characterizes the covenant will be present forever, even for the foreigner. The constant provision of hesed will never be limited by the sin of the people. It will even be there for those who are not his people, for the Gentiles (2 Chron 6:22-33).

The climax to Solomon's great poem of prayer comes in 2 Chronicles 6:41-42. It is nothing less than the formal invitation to the Lord to take up residence in the midst of his people, to come to rest. Solomon promises that those who are dependent on God's hesed (the Hebrew word is *hasidim*, or his "saints") will rejoice in his goodness. Finally, exhausted, Solomon cries out, "LORD God . . . remember your *hesed* for your servant David."

Chapter 7 opens with fire falling from heaven and the glory of the Lord filling the temple, a dramatic demonstration that the invitation of Solomon has been accepted (2 Chron 7:1). The God who has made a covenant of hesed with his people, the God whom all heaven cannot contain, takes up residence and comes to rest in Solomon's temple— for a time. As Solomon has so well sung, there never has been nor ever will be nor ever could be a God like the God of Israel.

The list of would-be rivals is endless. In Egypt the Israelites had encountered Horus, Amun, Isis, Serapis, Osiris, and Thoth. The ancient Egyptian Book of the Dead lists about five hundred gods, including gods half animal and half human, gods who were chopped up and thrown into the Nile, and gods who collected the pieces. There are few references in the Hebrew Scriptures to the Israelites being tempted to worship these gods. It's hard to find the time for that kind of temptation when you're busy making bricks. Still, the incident of the golden calf reveals they had been infected by Egyptian idolatry.

When they finally took the Promised Land, the Jews encountered an equally dizzying array of pagan deities. There was Baal, who the wicked Jezebel worshiped and King Ahab built a temple for (1 Kings 16:31; 2 Kings 10:18). Elijah dealt with Baal definitively on Mount Carmel in 1 Kings 18. Baal was known for demanding children to be sacrificed to him by fire.

Then there was the female deity Ashtoreth, also known in the Bible as Astarte. She demanded obscene sexual fertility rites. Lewd statues of her have been dug up all over Israel. She is commonly confused with Asherah, who was a separate deity. Asherah was worshiped by means of "fertility poles." In the books of Judges and Kings one of the principal activities of the Israelites was cutting these poles down.

Molech was a particularly gruesome demonic god, demanding that the Israelites cause their children to "pass through the fire" (Lev 18:21; Jer 32:35). His idol was a large bronze furnace with a ramp, down which helpless infants were rolled into the fire. Unimaginably, Solomon built an altar to Molech near Jerusalem, and it was for this that the kingdom was torn away from him and given to his son (1 Kings 11:7-13). The Hinnom valley outside Jerusalem was notorious as the place of worship of both Baal and Molech. One tradition says there was a continuous beating of the drums to drown out the infant screams. The valley was later used as a trash dump for the city, where fires continually smoldered. In the imaginations of the biblical writers "Hinnom" became an image for hell.

The list goes on: Dagon, the Philistine god whose temple Samson destroyed in Judges 16; Chemosh, for whom Solomon also built a temple (1 Kings 11:7); Milcom; Nergal; Marduk; and Kaiwan, the star god. And who could forget Nehushtan, the idol the Israelites made from the brass serpent the Lord used in saving them from the poisonous snakes in the wilderness (2 Kings 18:4).

After even a brief overview of the cruelty of these demonic pagan gods, it becomes clear why in 1 Chronicles 6:14 Ezra the scribe recorded Solomon's declaration of the absolute uniqueness of the God for whom he had built the temple:

> LORD God of Israel,
> there is no God like you
> in heaven or on earth,
> who keeps his covenant *and hesed*
> with your servants who walk before you
> with all their heart.

The God of Abraham, Isaac, and Jacob, the God who held back Abraham's hand at the binding of Isaac, the God of Exodus 34, created the world, the rabbis said, just so he could show it his *hesed*. After the first couple sinned in the garden, he sought them out in the cool of the evening to cover their disobedient nakedness with animal skins. He is both perfectly just and merciful. His children can always expect from him more forgiveness and mercy than they deserve.

Given the demands of the demonic gods for infant sacrifice, the story of Abraham and Isaac takes on a new light. You and I see that story as a proof of Abraham's faith and commitment to God, which it surely is. But is it not as much or more a story about the character of God? Could it not also be a dynamic story of God's powerful demonstration to Abraham that he was not like the other gods? At the very

moment Abraham is tempted to think his God is demanding the sacrifice of his firstborn, the miracle child, the Angel of the Lord stops
him. He had most likely presumed that this God was indeed like all
the other gods and demanded the sacrifice of children. Perhaps that
is why when the command first came, Abraham did not open his
mouth in protest. *This is what you do for the gods*, he must have thought
as he readied himself for the journey to Mount Moriah.

But now, out of breath on the mountaintop, his eyes are open to
the Lord, the God of hesed, who as Ezra says is not like the other gods.
He will not demand Isaac's blood. Unlike any other god he himself will
provide the sacrifice, as he will provide manna, living water, and
shoes that never wear out. Again and again, just when a multitude of
characters in the Bible realize their own inadequacy, their own sin,
just when they realize they have a right to expect nothing, they receive not simply a second chance but everything from God. A new age
of trusting the Lord is born.

Linguistic scholars have begun to believe that there is no cognate
in any other ancient language for the word *hesed*.[1] It is a uniquely
Hebrew word. Perhaps the reason for this is not linguistic but spiritual.
Perhaps the reason no other language possesses a word that can
capture the full meaning of *hesed* is that in all other cultures this particular idea never existed. There is a very good reason for the fact that
we possess no ancient hymns to the kindness of Baal or Molech or
Astarte or Osiris or Zeus or any of the other pagan gods.[2]

In the closing verses of his prophecy, Micah, looking forward to the
rise of Israel after the exile, says these amazing words:

> Who is a God like you,
>   forgiving iniquity and passing over rebellion
>   for the remnant of his inheritance?

He does not hold on to his anger forever
because he delights in *hesed*. (Mic 7:18)

Make no mistake, our world today is as full of idols, of false gods, as the world of the Hebrew Bible ever was. And they are worshiped and sacrificed to with as much zeal as ever Baal or Molech was. Fortunes are still poured out at their feet. The blood of innocent children is still offered up to them in quantities that would make an ancient pagan's head spin. But what set the God of Israel apart then, what made him completely unique to the point that the other gods were no gods at all, is what still sets him apart today. He is the God who delights in being kind, in loving his creation, and in offering forgiveness and salvation to those who have no right to expect anything from him.

The great surprise of the New Testament was that when God finally acted, he did so in the form of a slave. Jesus is crucified in weakness. He is sold for the price of a slave, dies the death of a slave. The great surprise of the Hebrew Bible is not that God is awesome or holy. These characteristics we would expect from God. The great surprise is that he is kind, that he is a God of hesed. This is what fundamentally makes him unlike any other god, then or now.

AN EVERLASTING REFRAIN

Give thanks to the LORD, for he is good;
his *hesed* endures forever.

1 CHRONICLES 16:34

Sitting in the back of an ancient church during one of my early tours of England, I discovered an old split-page hymnal. It's a complicated arrangement whereby you can have the bottom of a page open to one lyric and the top open to a different melody. Always on the lookout for lyrical ideas, I was skimming through the antique hymns. One caught my eye: "All praise to Thee, Who safe has kept, And hast refreshed me while I slept." *Hmmm,* I said to myself. And then, "Wert Thou not there to be enjoyed, And I in hymns to be employed." Given the old-timey nature of the language, I was unmoved. And then I read in the last verse:

> Praise God, from Whom all blessings flow
> Praise Him all creatures here below
> Praise Him above, ye heavenly host
> Praise Father, Son, and Holy Ghost.

Yikes! The Doxology! There it was, the last verse of a hymn that by comparison was pretty unremarkable. Yet the writer, Thomas Ken, had captured in the final verse perhaps the greatest contemporary words of praise ever written. They lay there, almost hidden, among other, less remarkable lyrics.

Something like that happens in 1 Chronicles 16. There we find a lengthy psalm, all holy Scripture, but from which one line was lifted (like the Doxology) that became a standard formula repeated throughout the Bible.

It is a challenge to the imagination to picture the scene. A procession extending for miles is composed of the faithful congregation of Israel, of musicians in white linen robes playing every sort of instrument. At the head of the procession the priests are carrying the ark of the covenant, safely suspended between two poles. And in the lead is the king himself, David, dancing or perhaps "whirling," caught up in the magnificence of the moment. The "ark of the testimony" that represents the presence of the Lord is finally coming home to Jerusalem. After the ark is placed in the tent shrine David has erected, a series of offerings are made, followed by an enormous civic meal. David provides for each person a loaf of bread and cakes of compressed dates and raisins.

Asaph, who has officially been appointed "giver of thanks" (or worship leader), proceeds to lead the priests and musicians in a hymn, presumably written by Asaph himself. It is directed at the people, calling on them to give thanks, to celebrate in praise to God, to search for him and remember his deeds and his covenant, and to declare his glory among the nations. As the song, sung by the priests, is coming to a close there is a description of the splendor and glory of the Lord, followed by a final charge to the people to give thanks. Then while the final notes echo away the crowd joyfully responds, "Amen," and "Praise the LORD" (1 Chron 16:36).

Tucked into this lengthy song is a line, a formula if you will. As far as I can tell this is the first time it was ever sung. Yet it would become central to the liturgy of Israel—Israel's new national motto (not unlike "in God we trust" in the United States). And it is based on the word *hesed*!

Give thanks to the LORD, for he is good;
his *hesed* endures forever. (1 Chron 16:34)

The next time we hear this refrain is in 2 Chronicles 5:13. Previously it was embedded in the middle of a lengthy song of praise. Now it is sung in isolation, precisely at one of the most significant moments in the history of ancient Israel.

Solomon, David's son, has finally completed the construction of the temple. Now the ark has been placed, not in a tent shrine but in the holy of holies. The entire Levitical chorus is standing before the temple with a full array of instruments: symbols, harps, lyres, and trumpets. The priestly choir and orchestra join in singing, not a lengthy song but one simple lyric:

For he is good;
his *hesed* endures forever.

In response to this perfect praise, the temple is filled with what Ezra first describes as a cloud, but then clarifies: "The glory of the LORD filled God's temple" (2 Chron 5:13-14).

Later, in 2 Chronicles 7:1, after Solomon concludes his dedicatory prayer, closing with a final reference to the hesed of his father David (2 Chron 6:42), fire rains down from heaven and consumes all the offerings and sacrifices. Once again the Lord's glory fills the temple. In response all the congregation falls on their faces and worships again with the words, "He is good, for his *hesed* endures forever" (2 Chron 7:3). (Ezra 3:11 reports that upon the completion of the foundations of the second temple after the return of the exiles, the descendants of Asaph sing this same lyric.)

This formula next appears in the historical books in 2 Chronicles 20. The setting is a battle. The Ammonite and Moabite armies have come to wage war against Judah. A Levite named Jahaziel has prophesied that the battle does not belong to the people, but to the Lord (2 Chron 20:14-15).

The next morning, as the men of Judah are preparing to go out to battle, Jehoshaphat encourages them to believe in the Lord and to trust his prophets. They will not wage war. They will simply sing. Can you guess what the lyric of their song is?

Give thanks to the LORD,
for his *hesed* endures forever. (2 Chron 20:21)

Before the congregation and their song, the enemy proceeds to turn on each other and annihilate one another.

A single line from a lengthy psalm is lifted to become the phrase that welcomes the glory of the Lord to the ark shrine and finally to the temple itself. Once we leave the historical writings we encounter this formula in a number of the Psalms: thirty-four times, to be precise. Twenty-six of those occurrences are in Psalm 136. That sacred formula, which celebrates the enduring nature of the hesed of God, became woven into the fabric of Israel's worship as their hearts resonated with the truth of who their God is.

With them were Heman, Jeduthun, and the rest who were chosen and designated by name to give thanks to the LORD—for his *hesed* endures forever. (1 Chron 16:41)

The trumpeters and singers joined together to praise and thank the LORD with one voice. They raised their voices, accompanied

by trumpets, cymbals, and musical instruments, in praise to
the LORD:

> For he is good;
> his *hesed* endures forever. (2 Chron 5:13)

All the Israelites were watching when the fire descended and the
glory of the LORD came on the temple. They bowed down on the
pavement with their faces to the ground. They worshiped and
praised the LORD:

> For he is good,
> for his *hesed* endures forever. (2 Chron 7:3)

The priests and the Levites were standing at their stations. The
Levites had the musical instruments of the LORD, which King
David had made to give thanks to the LORD—"for his *hesed* en-
dures forever"—when he offered praise with them. (2 Chron 7:6)

When they went out in front of the armed forces, they kept singing:

> Give thanks to the LORD,
> for his *hesed* endures forever. (2 Chron 20:21)

They sang with praise and thanksgiving to the LORD: "For he is
good; his *hesed* to Israel endures forever." Then all the people
gave a great shout of praise to the LORD because the foundation
of the LORD's house had been laid. (Ezra 3:11)

For the LORD is good, and his *hesed* endures forever;
his faithfulness, through all generations. (Ps 100:5)

Hallelujah!
Give thanks to the LORD, for he is good;
his *hesed* endures forever. (Ps 106:1)

Give thanks to the LORD, for he is good;

his *hesed* endures forever.

Let the redeemed of the LORD proclaim

that he has redeemed them from the power of the foe.

(Ps 107:1-2)

A sound of joy and gladness, the voice of the groom and the bride, and the voice of those saying,

Give thanks to the LORD of Armies,

for the LORD is good;

his *hesed* endures forever. (Jer 33:11)

Along with the vast range of meaning associated with the word *hesed*, now we must add that it is eternal, everlasting, indestructible. Without this facet, hesed would not be hesed. If it were based on a whim or a momentary feeling, it would not be hesed. If time could wear it down or wash it away, it would not be hesed. But it lasts forever, is ultimately reliable. It never changes. It can always be trusted in, relied upon, asked and hoped for.

What are the implications for us today of God's hesed being everlasting and eternal? What kind of confidence might be born in our hearts and minds if we trusted that God's love, mercy, and kindness will never fail, never leave us in the lurch? What would happen to our deepest lingering fears if we could summon the audacity to believe this promise, a promise that obviously meant so much to Israel?

A PRAYER OF HONEST RAGE

God of my praise, do not be silent.

For wicked and deceitful mouths open against me;
they speak against me with lying tongues.
They surround me with hateful words
and attack me without cause.
In return for my love they accuse me,
but I continue to pray.
They repay me evil for good,
and hatred for my love.

Set a wicked person over him;
let an accuser stand at his right hand.
When he is judged, let him be found guilty,
and let his prayer be counted as sin.
Let his days be few;
let another take over his position.
Let his children be fatherless
and his wife a widow.
Let his children wander as beggars,

searching for food far from their demolished homes.

Let a creditor seize all he has;

let strangers plunder what he has worked for.

Let no one show him *hesed*,

and let no one be gracious to his fatherless children.

Let the line of his descendants be cut off;

let their name be blotted out in the next generation.

Let the iniquity of his fathers

be remembered before the LORD,

and do not let his mother's sin be blotted out.

Let their sins always remain before the LORD,

and let him remove all memory of them from the earth.

For he did not think to show *hesed*,

but pursued the suffering, needy, and brokenhearted

in order to put them to death.

He loved cursing—let it fall on him;

he took no delight in blessing—let it be far from him.

He wore cursing like his coat—

let it enter his body like water

and go into his bones like oil.

Let it be like a robe he wraps around himself,

like a belt he always wears.

Let this be the LORD's payment to my accusers,

to those who speak evil against me.

But you, LORD, my Lord,

deal kindly with me for your name's sake;

because your *hesed* is good, rescue me.

For I am suffering and needy;

my heart is wounded within me.

I fade away like a lengthening shadow;

I am shaken off like a locust.

My knees are weak from fasting,

and my body is emaciated.

I have become an object of ridicule to my accusers;

when they see me, they shake their heads in scorn.

Help me, LORD my God;

save me according to your *hesed*

so they may know that this is your hand

and that you, LORD, have done it.

Though they curse, you will bless.

When they rise up, they will be put to shame,

but your servant will rejoice.

My accusers will be clothed with disgrace;

they will wear their shame like a cloak.

I will fervently thank the LORD with my mouth;

I will praise him in the presence of many.

For he stands at the right hand of the needy

to save him from those who would condemn him.

We usually skim or completely skip passages like Psalm 109. It does not belong in our modern world. It comes from a darker time. (As if there has ever been a time as dark as ours.) And after all, precisely because of hesed, aren't we supposed to love our enemies (Lk 6:27)?

Yet this is a psalm of hesed. The word occurs four times, in two negative examples and two positive. It is a psalm of David, who as we will see was a particular focus of hesed. If, like me, you've tended to pass by Psalm 109, then it is time to stop and look it squarely in the face. Perhaps we have not understood this psalm because we have violated the first commandment: to love God by listening (Deut 6:4-5).

If you pay close attention to Psalm 109, you will hear the anger of King David, who cares deeply for the poor. He mourns for them and with them and is outraged that an unnamed official, someone from his inner circle, someone David has actually loved and trusted, has violated that trust, has abused his authority, and, beyond all else, has failed to return the hesed that was shown to him.[1]

The psalm opens with David's plea to the Lord to speak up, to no longer remain silent. This parallels the next verse, where David points out that someone is speaking up against him. (Note also Psalm 83, of Asaph, which is another "enemy psalm" and opens with a similar plea to God to speak.) David petitions God to become involved in what is pictured as a courtroom scene, whether figurative or actual. David pleads to the God of Exodus 34 to enter into and share his outrage that someone who was shown hesed has willfully and intentionally chosen not to return that lovingkindness to those who need it most, the poor.

Verse 16 is the key that unlocks the psalm. The nameless guilty official pursued the suffering and brokenhearted, going so far as to murder them. The severity of his crime explains the imprecations of verses 6-15. Each curse hopes that what this person has done to the poor, God, the One who will not leave the guilty unpunished, will in his hesed allow to happen to him: that someone equally wicked will be placed over him, for that is what the poor experienced under his evil term of office; that his days will be few, even as the lives of poor people were cut short under his tenure; that his children and wife will suffer in ways similar to how poor women and children have suffered; that he will wander as a beggar; that his home will be torn down, as their homes were destroyed; that creditors will seize his possessions. All because "he did not think to show *hesed*" (Ps 109:16).

David had placed this nameless official in a position of power to help the poor, had shown him royal hesed. He responded with hatred and evil (Ps 109:5). It is not some sort of official covenant he has violated. After all, hesed does not come from covenant; covenant comes from hesed. This unnamed evil person has desecrated a loving relationship of trust. David's expectation had been based on the hope that hesed would be returned to the poor with whom he stands in solidarity.

This psalm is not simply poetic words in black and white on a page. It represents the raw emotions of someone whose heart has been broken and who mourns and rages that the poor have suffered in the process. David, in fact, radically identifies with the poor (Ps 109:22).

David has learned that the only place he can take these dark emotions, his sense of outrage, his righteous anger, is to the God of hesed, who does not leave the guilty unpunished. On the basis of God's lovingkindness, David makes his appeal for God to act. His plea is that the Lord will respond because he shares the same outrage, the same deep disappointment, the same solidarity with the poor.

Walter Brueggemann says that such rage belongs in our prayer lives.[2] If we understand and take seriously the God of hesed, along with David we will share the same outrage when those who have been given positions of power to help the suffering use that power to make themselves rich and abuse the poor in the process. In one sense they have become our enemies, whom Jesus himself says we must love (Mt 5:44; Lk 6:27, 35). But in order to love our enemies, we must first acknowledge that we *have* enemies and identify just who they are. Too often Jesus' radical command to love our enemies is watered down, reduced to a platitude. In fact, it is a fundamental demand, but it's impossible to accomplish without his mercy at work in us, his hesed becoming enfleshed in our lives.

Loving your enemies is a grueling task. The significant lesson we learn from David and Psalm 109 is that we do not take our anger and outrage to the streets or to Washington first, but to the One we hope and trust and believe cares more deeply for the poor than we ever will, even as at the same time he cares for our enemies. The failure to show hesed has consequences (Mt 5:7). When our hearts have been sufficiently transformed to feel the outrage, David teaches us to offer it up as an act of worship to the One who we trust is even more disappointed and outraged himself and who will act on behalf of the poor out of his just mercy, out of infinite and enduring hesed.

PART TWO

THE OBJECTS OF HESED

7

WHEN DINAH HELD MY HAND

Our small reconciliation group, the Empty Hands Fellowship, had been meeting for prayer for about a year. It was 1995. At the same time, my church had been trying different strategies to attract minorities to our almost completely white congregation. None of them was working. We were tired of the Sunday church hour being the most segregated hour of the week. It occurred to me that if our invitations were not bringing anyone in, perhaps we should reach out and visit some of the local black churches.

First Missionary Baptist is one of the oldest congregations in our town, founded in 1870, not long after the Civil War. The pastor, Denny Denson, was one of the leaders in Empty Hands. We had become friends during the time we had been meeting for prayer, first at Mc-Donald's and eventually at First Missionary. I thought I would begin by going there.

The first Sunday morning I visited, I was the only white person in the congregation. Still, I felt at home. We had been praying there on Wednesdays for several months, and I knew my way around. One elderly lady came up and greeted me with a warm smile. "Why are you here?" she innocently asked.

"I'm friends with Denny," I said. And that was good enough for her.

As the service began, I found a place a few pews from the back. The first song was "Jesus Is on the Main Line." I had never heard it before, but it became one of my favorites in the years that followed as I became a more regular part of the congregation. "Jesus is on the main line. Tell him what you want!"

Next to me was a large woman I had never met before. I later found out that she was the wife of Bob Smith, one of the members of Empty Hands. Her name was Dinah. After a few more songs, announcements, the reading of thank-you cards and letters, and a brief devotion provided by one of the deacons (Denny thought it was a good way to "keep them in the Word"), the pastor stepped up to the pulpit and began his sermon.

At that moment, without saying a word, Dinah reached across the pew and took my hand. I froze, not knowing what to do. I looked around to see if anyone else was holding hands. Maybe this was another tradition I was unfamiliar with. But no one else was. Whenever Denny would repeat the theme of his sermon, a popular device in black preaching, Dinah would give my hand a squeeze. She didn't let go until the service was over. As we stood to sing the benediction, she smiled at me and said she hoped I would be back.

I was mystified by the experience. At the next Empty Hands meeting I asked her husband, Bob, if that was her usual way of treating strangers. He smiled and shook his head. "You don't know the half of it," he said.

He told me that over the years he and Dinah had raised more than seventy-five foster children, both black and white. "I never knew when I came home from work if there was going to be another person at the table," he said. Now in his eighties, though he could have been enjoying retirement, Bob was bagging groceries at the local Kroger just to help out one of their adopted kids. When someone asked Dinah why she had opened her home in such an extravagant way, she responded simply, "If I don't love them, who else will?" That was Dinah Smith, someone I will never forget.

As I came to know her better over the years, I slowly began to understand what had happened that first morning at First Missionary. For a few moments I had entered into the gravitational field of Dinah's remarkable kindness. She had adopted me, had opened the door of her life to me. I had become an *object of her hesed*. I had done absolutely nothing to deserve her kindness. I had simply shown up with all my mixed motives. But she reached out to me and took my hand.

As a stranger, a white male, who might have represented a host of negative feelings, I had no right to expect anything from her that morning. Not a welcome or a greeting, and certainly not an affectionate holding of my hand. But if she didn't love me, who else was going to? In that old, simple church over twenty years ago Dinah Smith taught me what it means to become the object of hesed.[1]

When Dinah Held My Hand

She was haloed round in kindness
I was nervous and alone
A stranger come into her world
The church that was her home
But she'd been taught to love on strangers
As only the suffering can
That Sunday morning set me free
When Dinah held my hand

The service was about to start
It was my destiny
The only place beside her
Was waiting just for me
Without a word she reached across

And gently took my hand
And the path I've traveled ever since
That morning it began

Chorus

She reached out across three hundred years
Of suffering and pain
She reached out across the great divide
Of the color of our skins
When she reached out across the empty pew
Then I could understand
How the Lord was reaching out to me
When Dinah held my hand

She was strong and she was kind
But gentle when she spoke her mind
Cause Jesus is on the mainline
You can tell Him what you want
By the force of her own gravity
Her outrageous generosity
That morning I began to see
When she adopted me

Life is made of moments
We don't always understand
Sometimes the meaning isn't clear
Like there's no specific plan
But every moment has been set in place
Before the world began
Like the time that Sunday morning
When Dinah took my hand.[2]

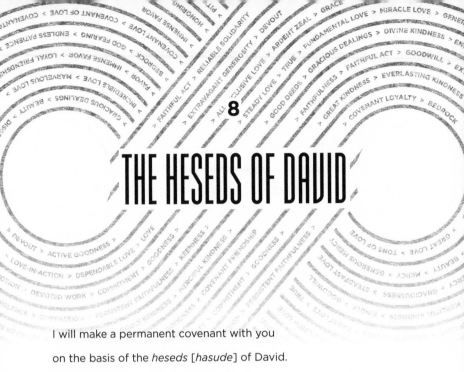

8

THE HESEDS OF DAVID

I will make a permanent covenant with you

on the basis of the *heseds* [*hasude*] of David.

ISAIAH 55:3

In chapter 55, Isaiah is still confident of the loyalty the Lord promised to David. That covenant remained the basis of Israel's hope two and a half centuries later. The invitation to those who are thirsty in the opening verse of Isaiah 55 will then echo forward in time almost one thousand years to Revelation 21:6. The God of David is the One who provided manna and living water in the wilderness and who through Isaiah promises water, milk, wine, and food to his people. These are the "kindnesses" of David named in verse 3, a rare use of the plural form of *hesed*.[1]

Hesed seems to have been a part of David's DNA. His great grandmother, the compassionate Moabite widow Ruth, was a paradigm of hesed. She selflessly gave her life to her mother-in-law, Naomi. She also received hesed from her husband, Boaz. Their genetic lovingkindness would eventually be passed down to Jesus. Matthew lists

Ruth as one of Jesus' ancestors (Mt 1:5). As Exodus 34 is the defining moment of hesed in the Hebrew Bible, so David is its definitive human representative in the Hebrew Bible.

Yet David seems to have grown up as a stranger to hesed. He lived a wilderness childhood, both literally and figuratively. We have hints of the abuse he experienced as a boy, the youngest of eight brothers (1 Sam 17:28). One of the most telling details of David's early life is that when the prophet Samuel came to Jesse, looking for the next anointed king of Israel, all of Jesse's sons were brought before Samuel before anyone thought to send for David, who was tending the flocks. Apparently it occurred to no one that the young boy might be a choice for king. David seems to have been perpetually overlooked and left out.

After the Goliath incident, Jonathan, the son of Saul, committed himself to David. According to 1 Samuel 18:1-3, Jonathan loved David as much as he loved himself. They were both fearless warriors, Jonathan no less than David (see 1 Sam 13:3; 14:1-14). In 1 Samuel 20:8, 14-17, the two initially enter into a covenant of hesed, a covenant to which David will remain faithful after Jonathan is killed.

Jonathan's faithfulness to David as the latter rose to prominence is itself a parable of hesed. David had no right to expect anything from Jonathan. Jonathan should have rightfully become king, though a specified process of succession was probably not in place yet. But Jonathan extends to David his faithful friendship to the very end of his tragic life. David's first experience of hesed is in the context of his extraordinary friendship with Jonathan.

THE RECIPROCITY OF HESED

The remarkable relationship between David and Jonathan best displays one of the fundamental facets of hesed, reciprocity.[2] Once a relationship or covenant of hesed is established there is an unspoken mutuality. The one who was initially shown hesed naturally demonstrates hesed in return. This is not a legal expectation; there are no covenant sanctions tied to it. Rather, an expectation based on hope is in view. To receive hesed and not return it leaves the initial party deeply disappointed, be it an individual or God himself.

This deep mutuality of hesed is powerfully demonstrated in the relationship between David and Jonathan. David says, "Deal *with hesed* with your servant, for you have brought me into a covenant with you before the LORD. If I have done anything wrong, then kill me yourself; why take me to your father?" (1 Sam 20:8).

Jonathan replies, "May the LORD be with you, just as he was with my father. If I continue to live, show me *hesed* from the LORD, but if I die, don't ever withdraw your *hesed* from my household—not even when the LORD cuts off every one of David's enemies from the face of the earth" (1 Sam 20:13-15).

Reciprocity is an indication that you have internalized the truth of hesed. If it is not returned freely in gratitude, you have not understood the nature of the hesed that was shown to you in the first place. (Note that Jesus' brother James speaks of this as well: "For judgment is without mercy to the one who has not shown mercy"; Jas 2:13.)

The expectation of mutuality is based not on strict obligation but on the hope that the one who received hesed will reciprocate. You have, in a sense, violated hesed if you fail to show hesed in response. Here are some examples of the reciprocal nature of hesed:

- Rahab expects and asks for hesed from Joshua and the spies because she did an act of hesed for them. (Josh 2:12)

- The spies scouting out the city of Bethel promise hesed to a man of the town if he shows them the way in. As a result they spare his family. (Judg 1:24)

- The Israelites fail to show hesed to Gideon though he had been kind to them. (Judg 8:35)

- Saul does not destroy the Kenites because they showed hesed to the Israelites when they came out of Egypt. (1 Sam 15:6)

- David sends word to the men of Jabesh-gilead that because they did hesed by burying the body of Saul the Lord will show hesed to them. (2 Sam 2:5)

- David shows hesed to Mephibosheth, the invalid son of Jonathan, because Jonathan showed hesed to David. (2 Sam 9:1, 3, 7)

- David shows hesed to Hanun because his father showed hesed to David. (2 Sam 10:2)

- David, on his deathbed, tells Solomon to show hesed to the sons of Barzillai because they supported David when he was fleeing Absalom. (1 Kings 2:7)

In each incident there is a clear hope that the act of hesed will be reciprocated and serious disappointment when it is not. Hesed cannot be the subject of a demand, just as love cannot be coerced because of a covenant. A man and a woman first fall in love and only then enter into the covenant of marriage; their covenant is born from their love. The hope that love will be shown in return is based not on a covenantal or formal legal agreement but rather on the hope that the initial recipient of hesed has integrated kindness into his or her way of life.

It is like the subtle nuance between a command and a commandment. A commandment implies a covenant agreement. If it is violated, there are penalties that automatically come into play, even as there are blessings that accompany obedience to the covenant. A command, on the other hand, connotes the presence of a person, a lord, who issues an order. If it is violated, the one who gave the command is disappointed. A relationship has been violated. The penalty, if you can call it that, is disappointing someone you revere.

The teaching of Jesus, particularly in Matthew's Gospel, is full of this particular notion of reciprocity, based on relationship and founded in hope:

- "Blessed are the merciful, / for they will be shown mercy" (Mt 5:7).

- "And forgive us our debts, / as we also have forgiven our debtors" (Mt 6:12).

- "For if you forgive others their offenses, your heavenly Father will forgive you as well. But if you don't forgive others, your Father will not forgive your offenses" (Mt 6:14-15).

- "Shouldn't you also have had mercy on your fellow servant, as I had mercy on you?" (Mt 18:33).

The hope of reciprocity is born out of relationship and is motivated by gratitude. We extend mercy and offer forgiveness as followers of Jesus, not to manipulate some sort of system whereby we expect to receive something in return but because we have been the recipients of his mercy and respond from a sense of gratitude to him. Jesus' teaching does not represent a strictly legal system where God forgives us because we forgave, quid pro quo. What a horrifying notion that God's forgiveness might be limited by our inability to forgive. No, God's forgiveness and mercy represent the gift of someone who, though we have no right to expect anything from him, still gives us all things. Before the relationship of hesed, we have no expectations, but after it is extended and received, everything changes.[3] Given this extravagant gift, how could we not respond in kind?

"ACCORDING TO . . ."

Jonathan's friendship and the hesed David experienced through him might well be the bright point of an otherwise stressful life, but David's disastrous affair with Bathsheba is certainly the low point of his life. Still, this failure provided an opportunity for him to learn more of and experience the hesed of God. Second Samuel 11–12 tells the story. In a matter of days David committed a long line of sins: adultery, murder, and lying. As a result of their affair Bathsheba (who is always referred to as "Uriah's wife") gives birth to a baby boy, who is fatally ill.

David goes into full mourning, fasting and pleading with God for the baby who he knows is suffering the consequences of his sin. He becomes so unhinged that all he can do is lie on the ground, refusing to eat. On the seventh day the child dies, one day short of receiving his name. David hears the whispering of the servants, who are afraid to tell him what has happened. He asks straightforwardly, "Is the baby dead?" To which they darkly respond, "He is dead" (2 Sam 12:19).

What happens next puzzled David's servants then and should puzzle us to this day, if we are listening to the text. David gets up from the ground, washes, eats, changes clothes, and goes to the temple. When the servants finally summon the courage to ask about his disturbing clarity, David responds with the words you often hear today at infant funerals: "I'll go to him, but he will never return to me" (2 Sam 12:23).

Some scholars believe that David wrote Psalm 51 as he was pleading with God for the life of the child. The psalm contains the explanation for David's otherwise inexplicable turnaround. As he writhed on the floor, David remembered the nature of the God of hesed, the same One who established his throne on hesed (1 Kings 3:6). Having ruined his life and that of Bathsheba, having taken the life of the noble Uriah and in effect the life of the nameless seven-day-old, David realizes that if he is to ever have a clean heart once again, if he is ever to be cleansed, it must be Someone else who will do the cleansing.

What David has done is unforgivable, but David can be forgiven—but only "according to" hesed. The person who has a right to expect nothing realizes in the midst of his mourning that he can ask boldly to receive what he does not deserve: cleansing, a clean heart, and a new life. David understands that he needs hesed the most when he deserves it the least.

> Be gracious to me, God,
> according to your *hesed*;
> according to your abundant compassion,
> blot out my rebellion. (Ps 51:1)

David is not the first person in Scripture to ask for forgiveness according to God's hesed. As we might expect, Moses was the first person to realize that he could ask that the people be forgiven in this way: "Please pardon the iniquity of this people, in keeping with the greatness of your *hesed*" (Num 14:19). It is something that unites these two superstars of the Bible. They both knew God so intimately that they understood that they could ask for and expect to receive precisely what they did not deserve (compare Lk 7:1-9).

From the opposite perspective we might ask, Do you really want what you deserve? If we think about it, the answer would certainly be no! I most definitely do not want what I deserve. I desire most what I definitely do not deserve. David's life teaches us that we can ask, beg, and expect to receive according to the standard of God's hesed. Hesed has become a standard that we can appeal to. God invites us to expect more from him than we have a right to deserve.

An expectation based in hope that the kindness we have received will be returned by us in gratitude. The confidence that we can ask for and expect infinitely more than we deserve: forgiveness, grace, and restoration. David incarnates these lessons for us as no one else in the Hebrew Scriptures does.

9

ETHAN

"I WILL SING"

I will sing about the LORD's *hesed* [*hasude*] forever.

PSALM 89:1

The Bible presents many puzzling pieces of the life of Ethan the Ezrahite, the composer of Psalm 89. Jeremiah (the traditional author of 1 Kings) says that Solomon was even wiser than Ethan (1 Kings 4:31). Comparing someone to Solomon, the wisest man in the world, would be like introducing someone today as being wiser than Einstein. But Ethan's great wisdom is only the first tantalizing piece.

In 1 Chronicles 15:17, 19, Ezra (the traditional author) mentions Ethan, Heman, and Asaph being appointed as musicians, specifically as cymbal players, to perform with an orchestra of many other Levites. They made music as the ark was returned to Jerusalem, with David "whirling" in his fine linen robe and ephod at the front of the miles-long procession. Only Saul's daughter, Michal, seems to have refused to join in the celebration (1 Chron 15:29).

To add to the mystery, there is a good chance that Ethan was known by another name, Jeduthun. If this is true, there are two other psalms that are uniquely connected with him, 62 and 77. The enigma is that they are not said to have been written by him, but rather assigned to him. We don't know precisely what this means.

According to 1 Chronicles 2:6, one of Ethan's five brothers was Heman. He composed Psalm 88, which occurs just before the psalm Ethan wrote. Psalm 88 is unique among the lament psalms in that it laments all the way to the end. There is no resolve to praise as with every other psalm of lament. Ethan's Psalm 89 is unique in its own way: it begins with praise and transitions to lament. Both musicians are described as "Ezrahites," which is probably a reference to their father, Zerah.

If indeed Ethan and Jeduthun are the same person, one final fascinating piece of the puzzle comes to us in 1 Chronicles 16:41. Here it says Jeduthun and others were chosen and designated by name to give thanks to the Lord (and then comes our formula) "for his *hesed* endures forever." This mysterious, shadowy figure, whose wisdom was comparable to Solomon's, who wrote one of the Psalms and is enigmatically connected to two more, Ethan the Ezrahite, was chosen to sing about the eternal hesed of the Lord. It was his assigned theme, a part of his job description! Some solid evidence, a lot of conjecture, the truth is we still know virtually nothing about Ethan.

What we can say with confidence about him we learn from the opening verse of his psalm. It matches beautifully with our evidence, his job description, but more importantly it tells us about his heart. In verse one he pledges, "I will sing about the LORD's *hesed* forever" (Ps 89:1; see also Ps 101:1). If the formula is true and the Lord's hesed is eternal, then the only choice is to sing about it forever. Having put two and two together, that is exactly what Ethan proposed to do with the rest of his life.

Psalm 89 is a fascinating pledge to the eternal covenant of hesed given to David in 2 Samuel 7:15. In Ethan's song *hesed* appears seven times (and the word *throne* appears five times). It is a lyric to the establishment of David's throne. The musical promise is that David's throne will last forever, like God's hesed. (The word *forever* occurs eight times.)

Then in verse 38 there is an abrupt shift. So abrupt, in fact, that some scholars believe the song originally ended at verse 37. At verse 38 a lament begins because the outcome of David's kingdom did not seem to line up with the unparalleled success promised in the first thirty-seven verses. The psalm becomes extremely dark. Verse 46 echoes Psalm 13, with the cry, "How long?" The song reaches its lowest point in verse 49, where the question comes, "Lord, where are the former acts of your *hesed*?" The song limps along to the end, where there is a final note of eternal praise and a double "amen" that marks the close of one of the five books of Psalms.

An enigmatic character given a difficult assignment: to sing about the eternal hesed of God that, for the moment at least, does not appear to be so eternal. One of Zerah's two song-writing sons laments in a unique way about the lovingkindness of God and of his chosen, David. While we might simply say, "Well, it was his job to do so," there is much more going on beneath the lyrics and the history. The question might best be put: If the historical facts seem to deny the truth of the eternal nature of the *hesed* of God, why do Ethan and Heman and David and Solomon and Asaph and the sons of Korah sing about it nonetheless? Why can they not seem to keep themselves from singing about it? For that matter, why does anyone sing about it?

Singing involves resonance. Air passes through the vocal chords, causing them to resonate at a specific pitch. So too a string that is struck or plucked or hammered resonates at a specific, pre-tuned pitch. If you strike a C tuning fork and hold it next to a guitar string that is tuned to C, the string will begin to vibrate all by itself. In physics this is called "sympathetic resonance." And that is precisely why Ethan the Ezrahite sang about the eternal hesed of God.

Ethan was created in the image of the God of hesed (like you and me). Whenever his heart was struck or plucked or hammered by the thought of hesed, it resonated precisely at that pitch because it had been pre-tuned (created) to do so. When we see an act of hesed, an act where someone who has a right to expect nothing is nevertheless given everything, all of the sudden there are tears in our eyes, some sort of inexplicable resonance in our hearts, maybe even the beginnings of a song. Despite the overwhelming evidence all around us that kindness, love, mercy, and grace are a fragile tissue, a delusion, when we see one of those rare evidences of hesed, something, everything, within us resonates.

David's reign ends not with a bang but a whimper; nevertheless Ethan's heart continues to sing about the hesed that lasts forever. The temple lies in ruins, and Jeremiah still sings about the abundance of God's hesed (Lam 3:22, 32). Hesed is a deep vestigial part of the image of God in us. At even the darkest moments in our lives, when hesed seems most distant and least eternal, we find it somewhere in ourselves to sing about the reality of it, the eternality of it, or even the momentary abundance of it.

All of this explains why the vast majority of references that contain the word *hesed*, even those outside the psalter, are sung or occur in poems. The song of Moses sang about it in Exodus 15:13. David sang about it as he danced before the Lord in 1 Chronicles 16:34. Solomon sang about it when he dedicated the temple (1 Kings 8:23; 2 Chron 6:14). The people sang about it as the Spirit filled the new temple (2 Chron 7:3). God delivered the people as they sang about it, and the Ammonites and Moabites turned on each other (2 Chron 20:21). When the new foundations for the second temple were completed, the people sang about it (Ezra 3:11). When the Israelites confessed their sins as a nation in the time of Nehemiah, they sang about it (Neh 9:17, 32). The prophets would sing about the eternal nature of the Lord's hesed and the fragility of human hesed (Is 40:6; 54:8, 10; Jer 2:2; 31:3; Hos 2:19). At the birth of Jesus, Mary and Zechariah would sing about it (Lk 1:50, 54, 72, 78). Hesed is not sung only in the Psalms; all of these examples occur outside the Psalms. Hesed is something you sing about!

When we return to the Psalms, to the domain of people like Ethan, we hear not simply the note of hesed, but rather an entire symphony. Here are a few paraphrased examples of some of the resonances of hesed in the psalter:

- Psalm 5: I enter your house because of hesed.

- Psalm 6: You save me because of your hesed.

- Psalm 13: I trust in your hesed.

- Psalm 17: Display the wonders of your hesed.

- Psalm 18: He shows hesed to his anointed.

- Psalm 21: The king relies on the Lord's hesed.

- Psalm 23: Goodness and hesed will follow me all the days of my life.

- Psalm 25: Lord, remember your hesed; forget my sins in keeping with your hesed.

- Psalm 31: I will rejoice in your hesed. Save me by your hesed.

- Psalm 32: The one who trusts in the Lord will have hesed.

- Psalm 33: Let your hesed rest on us.

- Psalm 36: Your hesed reaches to heaven.

- Psalm 40: Your hesed and truth will guard me.

- Psalm 44: Redeem us because of your hesed.

- Psalm 48: We contemplate your hesed.

- Psalm 52: God's hesed is constant. I trust in God's hesed.

- Psalm 62: Hesed belongs to the Lord.

- Psalm 63: Hesed is better than life.

- Psalm 69: In your hesed you answer me with salvation. Your hesed is good.

- Psalm 85: Hesed and truth join together.

- Psalm 89: I will sing about hesed forever. I will declare hesed is built up forever.

- Psalm 94: Your hesed will support me.

- Psalm 98: He has remembered his hesed.

- Psalm 100: His hesed endures for all generations.

- Psalm 103: He crowns you with hesed and compassion. His hesed is toward those who fear him.

- Psalm 119: May your hesed comfort me. Give me life according to your hesed.

- Psalm 143: In your hesed destroy my enemies.

- Psalm 144: God is my hesed and fortress.

- Psalm 147: The Lord values those who put their trust in his hesed.

In the end, we return to enigmatic Ethan. He has sung all that he had in his heart to sing. He has sung of David and his eternal throne, founded on hesed. Though for the moment it all seems to have come to nothing, Ethan nevertheless sings. Despite the evidence, his God-shaped, hesed-tuned heart resonates. The truth of his song lies deeper than the superficial, fleeting evidence of the disaster of David's reign. The truth is, David's favor never depended on David in the first place, but on the One who, though David had no right to expect anything, gave him everything. Most especially he gave him an heir, a "Son," who would incarnate and extend hesed as a gracious gift to the world.

A song is a fragile, incomplete incarnation of an idea. Yet it can be an attempt to express what is otherwise inexpressible. To sing about hesed from a resonating heart is usually better than merely talking about it. If in a given situation you cannot "do" hesed, the choice still remains to sing about it and to the One who delights in it.

Ethan seemed to understand this as well as any of the psalmists. He could not fix what had gone wrong in David's reign, but nevertheless he could still sing, and could in fact sing about hesed *forever*. In the meantime, while you and I are wrestling with all that hesed means and pondering just how it should be done, with certainty we know we can sing of it and celebrate in song the God of hesed.

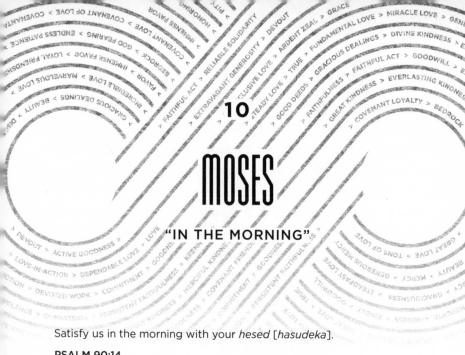

10

MOSES

"IN THE MORNING"

Satisfy us in the morning with your *hesed* [*hasudeka*].

PSALM 90:14

On our hesed-themed trip through Israel, our small group had been learning a bit of Hebrew, just enough to confuse the gracious Israelis who are always ready to help. One of the first phrases we learned was *boker tov*, which means "good morning." Our bus driver, Kamal, taught us that the appropriate response was the solemn and beautiful phrase *boker or*, which functionally means, "You have a good morning too." Literally, however, it means "morning of light." Begin your day with an experience that involves light. It would have been an appropriate response for Moses. He knew some of the best things from God come in the morning.[1]

Of the many words that *hesed* draws to itself by means of its linguistic gravity, *morning* is one that rarely makes any of the lists.

"I will . . . joyfully proclaim / your *hesed* in the morning" (Ps 59:16).

"It is good . . . to declare your *hesed* in the morning" (Ps 92:1-2).

"Let me experience / your *hesed* in the morning" (Ps 143:8).

In contrast to the hesed of God, Hosea says human hesed vanishes like mist in the morning (Hos 6:4).

Moses is no longer in the cleft of the rock, listening to those luminous words from God. Now he is a tired and disillusioned leader. The disastrous rebellion of Korah has taken place (Num 16). As best we can reconstruct the life situation of Psalm 90, Moses is in the wilderness of Zin, a strikingly beautiful area of deep gorges. His sister, Miriam, has just died (Num 20:1). In just a few verses his brother, Aaron, who except for a few lapses has been Moses' principal support in the wilderness, will also pass away. This is the setting for Psalm 90, the only psalm we have from Moses himself.[2]

When you engage the psalm with this background in mind it comes to life.

Lord, you have been our refuge
in every generation.
Before the mountains were born,
before you gave birth to the earth and the world,
from eternity to eternity, you are God.

You return mankind to the dust,
saying, "Return, descendants of Adam."
For in your sight a thousand years
are like yesterday that passes by,
like a few hours of the night.
You end their lives; they sleep.
They are like grass that grows in the morning—
in the morning it sprouts and grows;
by evening it withers and dries up.

For we are consumed by your anger;
we are terrified by your wrath.

You have set our iniquities before you,
our secret sins in the light of your presence.
For all our days ebb away under your wrath;
we end our years like a sigh.
Our lives last seventy years
or, if we are strong, eighty years.
Even the best of them are struggle and sorrow;
indeed, they pass quickly and we fly away.
Who understands the power of your anger?
Your wrath matches the fear that is due you.
Teach us to number our days carefully
so that we may develop wisdom in our hearts.

LORD—how long?
Turn and have compassion on your servants.
Satisfy us in the morning with your *hesed*
so that we may shout with joy and be glad all our days.
Make us rejoice for as many days as you have humbled us,
for as many years as we have seen adversity.
Let your work be seen by your servants,
and your splendor by their children.
Let the favor of the Lord our God be on us;
establish for us the work of our hands—
establish the work of our hands! (Ps 90)

This is a song from a person who knows about wandering in the wilderness, literally but also emotionally and spiritually. The opening verses speak of refuge and of mountains being born. In verses three, four, and five, Moses has the recent deaths of his two siblings clearly in mind. He writes with a poet's pen as his heart resonates with fresh grief. There is an imaginative play on words between the Hebrew word for dust (*adamah*) and the name Adam. "You return the descendants of Adam to the *adamah*," Moses laments.

How many memories are swirling through his mind when he says, "You end their lives; they sleep" (Ps 90:5)? In the following verses we hear the echoes of his wilderness experience, of being terrified by the wrath of God (Ps 90:7-11). In light of the death of Aaron and Miriam, Moses seems to be calculating the number of years he might have left. He speaks of hoping for eighty years but would settle for seventy. (He lived to be one hundred.)

Then Moses exits his reverie with a question that echoes throughout the Psalms: "How long?" He pleads with God to turn and show *rachamim* (mercies; Ps 90:13). He asks with the same confidence he first discovered on the mountain in Exodus 34. Finally, the connections we have been waiting to hear him speak about come to the surface. "Satisfy us in the morning with your *hesed*."

The word translated "satisfy" comes from *shavah* and usually refers to being satisfied with food. In Moses' imagination, hesed is something that satisfies a person's deep inner appetite. Perhaps Moses is remembering another time when his hunger was satisfied at daybreak, when in the wilderness the manna would miraculously appear to feed the multitude "in the morning" (Ex 16:13). *Manna* is a fascinating word in and of itself. *Ma* means "what" and is sometimes translated with a question mark. "*Na*," the particle of entreaty, means "oh" or perhaps "please." Sometimes it's translated with an exclamation mark. A creative translation of *manna* might be "?!" The satisfaction of hunger, manna, and morning were concepts that were woven together in Moses' mind.

Here, for the first of many examples, hesed and the morning appear together. It is striking that the lyricist is the same person who stood, covered by the kind hand of God, *in the morning* in Exodus 34, and heard that his hesed was extended to thousands. It touches the heart that this particular psalmist, among all others, would sing about the morning as a time when his appetite would be filled, not with manna that lasts only for a day but with hesed that is everlasting. The connections therefore are between morning, manna, hunger, and hesed.

Two final associations need to be made. First, in the New Testament, can you remember what image is connected to the manna in the wilderness? And when was that image actualized? The answers are profoundly simple. It is Jesus who is the living bread that came from heaven, the true manna (Jn 6:35). He is the One who promises to permanently satisfy our deepest hunger (Jn 6:48-51).

In addition, the Gospels all seem to be preoccupied with the fact that the resurrection of Jesus occurred *in the morning*, that time when there is just enough light to begin to see things clearly. From that morning on, his followers would experience the satisfaction of their deepest hunger by taking in the nourishment of that Living Bread that was first encountered in the morning. The Bread, who was the person who had incarnated every hope that hesed promises, rose, was seen, and was first embraced in the morning. Because of the resurrection of the living Manna that dawn, everything is new. And though you and I have a right to expect nothing, everything is freely given to us, every morning.

Could the tired and disheartened prophet, suffering the loss of his siblings, have ever imagined all of the connections he was making as he lamented, as he offered up his confusion and weariness as an act of worship in the wilderness? Was the ecstasy of that long-ago revelation still resonating somewhere deep down in his weary heart? Did he make the connection that the hesed he was pleading to be satisfied with had first dawned on him on the mountaintop in the morning? "Be prepared *by morning*," God had said. "Come up Mount Sinai *in the morning* and stand before me" (Ex 34:2, emphasis added).

Making connections between biblical words and passages is interesting and meaningful, but somewhere along the way they need to
intersect with daily life. Our lives are lived *daily*, and every single day
begins with a morning. To begin every day being satisfied, as Moses
says, with the lovingkindness of God, to experience that hesed every
morning as David sings in Psalm 143:8, is the most profound application imaginable. Any day that begins with such a realization will be
shaped by the kindness and hope that only the hesed of God can
bring. Every encounter that awaits in the day that follows such
mornings will be transformed and transformative.

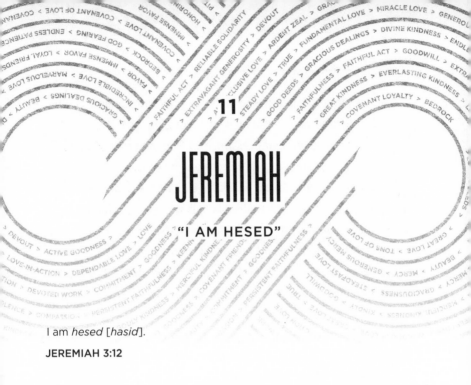

11

JEREMIAH

"I AM HESED"

I am *hesed* [*hasid*].

JEREMIAH 3:12

The word *hesed* occurs only some twenty-eight times in all the prophetic literature. (In contrast, it occurs twenty-six times in Psalm 136 alone!) The temptation might be to conclude that the prophets are less about God's lovingkindness and more about his judgment and anger. This kind of thinking has led to false differentiation between the angry God of the Old Testament and the loving God of the New. In reality the prophets provide their own unique contribution to our understanding of the word *hesed*, which was born out of the testing ground of six grueling centuries of the prophetic era (1020–400 BC).

In the Torah we discovered the definitive experience of God's hesed: God telling us who he is. In the historical books we witnessed the heartbreak associated with the violation of the hope of hesed. In the Psalms we listened to the unique resonance of the hesed our hearts were created and tuned to sing to. In the Prophets we meet the One who is himself hesed (Jer 3:12).[1]

The Prophets provide a portrait of the One who relentlessly reaches out to his people, who sends prophets like Jeremiah who weep and warn and plead with the people for decades before finally allowing the consequences of their sin to come into effect. It is the ultimate act of hesed, the final effort to redeem and restore his stubborn people, to whom he wants to open the door of his life.

Jeremiah's ministry extended over the reign of five kings, only one of whom (Josiah) actually listened to him. For over forty years he pleaded with the people to return. In Jeremiah chapters 3 and 4 the call to return echoes five times. That is all they need to do: simply come back to the One who is ready to forgive and restore and generously reward. But the people stubbornly refuse. Jeremiah is ridiculed. They compose derisive songs about him. His life is threatened over and over again. Ultimately, he is destroyed by the destruction he prophesied and is forced to witness the unthinkable devastation of the temple by the Babylonians in 586 BC (Jer 52; Dan 5). He remains behind in Jerusalem as the exiles depart. It will be seventy years before the people return and rebuild the temple.

Jeremiah does not simply use the word *hesed* more frequently than the other prophets; his writings also display many of the unique facets we have seen of the word:

- In Jeremiah 32:18, we hear the precise echo of Exodus 34:5-7 (see also Jer 16:10-13).

- In Jeremiah 33:11, we have an example of the formula of everlasting refrain.

- In two passages, Jeremiah 9:24 and 16:5, we see the force of *hesed*'s unique linguistic gravity as the words justice, righteousness, and compassion are drawn to it.

- In Lamentations 3:22, we see *hesed* functioning as the unique turning point between lament and praise (compare Ps 13:5; 69:13, 16).

- In Jeremiah 2:2, we see the fragileness of human hesed.

Throughout his writings we see the heartbreaking effect of the violation of the expectation, based in hope, that God's gracious hesed will be reciprocated by his people. Sadly, it never is.

This brings us finally to the ultimate expression of hesed in the writings of Jeremiah, and some would say in the entire Hebrew Bible. Given the fact that God has reached out to the people through his faithful, weeping prophet, that he has lovingly called out to them to return, that he has threatened inevitable destruction as the consequence of their stubborn disbelief, the hesed of God leaves him with only one option: he will keep the covenant they broke. In fact, God will establish a new covenant with both Israel and Judah. He will put his teaching in them; he himself will write it on their stubborn hearts. He will forgive and forget their sin (Jer 31:31-34).

As a visible, living, breathing incarnation of his hesed, God will send his "Righteous Branch." His name will be "The LORD Is Our Righteousness" (Jer 23:5-6). The Lord will be their righteousness—not their observances, not their meticulous "obediences." His righteousness will be given as a gift to those who have no right to expect anything from him. He will give them everything, most especially himself. He will do justice by loving and demonstrating hesed. And they and we will look back on all the consequences of our sin and see that his loving allowance of suffering for sin was perhaps the greatest expression of his hesed. Then all the suffering, all the confusion, all the tears will give birth to a new, unheard-of boast in Israel. This new exclamation will not involve the people's possession of the temple, nor their wisdom, strength, or wealth.

> But the one who boasts should boast in this:
> that he understands and knows me—
> that I am the LORD, showing *hesed*,
> justice, and righteousness on the earth,
> for I delight in these things. (Jer 9:24)

The context of Jeremiah specifically and the Prophets in general is one of stubborn disbelief and disobedience among God's people and of his persistent reaching out to them because of his hesed. In light of our inability to keep any of the covenants, God will graciously grant to us a new covenant, based solely on his faithfulness. That covenant will come into effect and be sustained by means of a person identified in Jeremiah as the Righteous Branch. We see hesed incarnated through the One who says that he himself is hesed.

In our New Testament way of thinking we call this new covenant a covenant of *grace*: God's Riches At Christ's Expense. At least that is the way I learned it in Sunday school. Like the covenant with Abraham, this new covenant is unconditional. It is not like the covenant that was made through Moses. Jeremiah 31:32 points out the contrast. This covenant will be actualized by God himself. He will place the teaching in our hearts. He will forgive and forget our sin (Jer 31:34). The context of the new covenant is clearly a product of God's lovingkindness. It is eternal and forever to be relied on.

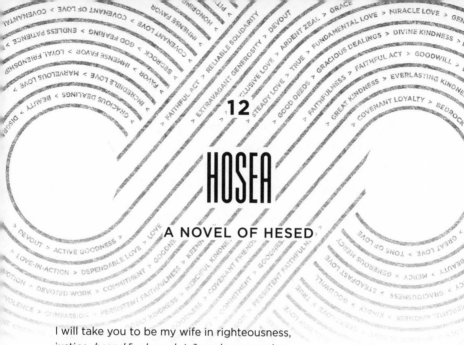

12

HOSEA

A NOVEL OF HESED

I will take you to be my wife in righteousness,
justice, *hesed* [*vahesedote*], and compassion.

HOSEA 2:19

There is no truth, no *hesed*,
and no knowledge of God in the land!

HOSEA 4:1

Your *hesed* [*vhasdkam*]
is like the morning mist.

HOSEA 6:4

For I desire *hesed* and not sacrifice.

HOSEA 6:6

Sow righteousness for yourselves
and reap *hesed*.

HOSEA 10:12

Maintain *hesed* and justice,
and always put your hope in God.

HOSEA 12:6

Hosea is a novel or a parable or a play or a dream or a nightmare, or perhaps even an incarnation. It is a dramatic reenactment of the love the Lord has for Israel, his wayward people. If you don't shed a tear or two when you read it, you're not listening with all of your "muchness," as the Shema commands us to do (Deut 6:4-5). If you don't engage with Hosea's emotional turmoil in the opening chapters of the book, the impossibility of what he was called to do, you've missed the point. The purpose behind the parable of Hosea and Gomer's life is to provide a window into the broken and betrayed heart of God, who will not give up on his people because of his hesed. Hosea's name is the secret key to the book, the dead giveaway. It means "salvation," the radical application and working out of God's lovingkindness.

It is not the call to marry Gomer, the prostitute, that is impossible, but the demand that she be loved in spite of her ongoing unfaithfulness. Though she has no right to expect anything from Hosea, he will lavish everything on her. Their relationship will incarnate the meaning of hesed.[1]

The parable of unfaithfulness is extended through the names of the three children Gomer bears to Hosea. The first, a boy named Jezreel, "God sows," will recall the bloodshed that occurred in the Jezreel Valley in 2 Kings 9:16–10:11. The second, a girl named Lo-ruhamah or "no mercy," will be a living representative of the fact that the Lord is fed up for the moment and intends to stop showing his compassion (*racham*) to his people. (Remember that *racham* is one of the words *hesed* frequently draws to itself.) The third child will bear the most despairing name: Lo-ammi, "not my people" (Hos 1:3-9).

There is an abrupt turn in verse 10, the same kind of transition we see in the psalms of lament, for it is God himself who is lamenting here. (Hosea 2:23 describes how the situation will be radically reversed.) The God of hesed will have compassion on the one who is identified as "No-compassion." To those who were "Not-my-people," he will affirm that indeed they *are* his people.

After the first three chapters, with their portrayals of Hosea's troubled relationship with Gomer, the book turns into a series of cycles, each one representing and amplifying the second half of God's revelation in Exodus 34:7: he will not leave the guilty unpunished. Hosea 10:10 pretty well sums it up: "I will discipline them."

Hesed continues to gravitationally draw familiar words to itself, such as justice, truth, and compassion (Hos 2:19; 4:1). We will see the word used the way the prophets usually use it, pointing out all that is lacking in the *hesed* of God's people (Hos 4:1; 6:4). It will function as an abrupt turning point in Hosea 10:12. And finally, in Hosea 12:6 the prophet will speak of what God's people must do to return to him. They must return and maintain hesed, justice, and hope in God (see also 3:5, 14:1).

Finally, the most quoted verse from Hosea is 6:6. Given the life situation of the book, it is remarkable that this single verse would eventually be used to reshape the faith of Israel after the destruction of the temple in AD 70.

The rabbis provide a remarkable story about Yohanan ben Zakkai and his pupil Yehoshua as they were leaving the smoldering ruins of Jerusalem. Joseph, the younger, lamented, "There is no longer a source of holiness in Israel." If you stop and think about it, he was right. If your religion dictates that you offer sacrifices in one single location, and that location is destroyed and you are forever banned as a people from returning, everything is indeed over.

In response ben Zakkai said, "We have a greater source of holiness." And then he quoted Hosea 6:6, "I desire *hesed* and not sacrifice" (Avot de Rabbi Natan 4). Ben Zakkai would go on to become one of the great reformers of post-temple Judaism in the city of Javneh, stressing acts of hesed over sacrifices. At that moment the seed was planted for what would eventually become Hasidic Judaism—that is, a Judaism founded on works of hesed, comprising a community that was completely dependent on the hesed of God.

A frustrated prophet gives his life in what appears to be an impossible call to love an unlovable person. Could he have ever dreamed that of the 209 verses in his prophecy, this single verse would affect the lives of millions of Jews and the millions more of us who have been grafted into that tree?

Years ago I was drawn into the world that is hesed by Hosea's frustrating book. Without knowing it, I was attempting to lyrically express the world of hesed in a song simply titled "Gomer's Song":

The fondness of a Father
The passion of a child
The tenderness of a loving friend
An understanding smile
All of this and so much more
You lavished on a faithless whore
I've never known love like this before
Hosea, you're a fool.

In the song I tried to put myself in Gomer's place in an effort to engage with the book in my imagination, trying to be as honest as I could. I imagined not that she would realize how precious the gift was that she was being offered, but that in the end she would conclude that Hosea was a fool for loving her the way he did. It seemed truer to the sparse picture of her in the book.

A fool to love someone like me
A fool to suffer silently
But somewhere through your eyes I see
I'd rather be a fool.[2]

I did grant her the hope of the remote possibility of a turnaround in that last line. But by every indication in the text, Gomer continued being herself, perpetually unfaithful and incapable of innocence.

But the book of Hosea is not about any kind of change in Gomer's heart. It's a book about God's heart, so full of the hesed he has pledged to show to thousands of generations. He longs for the people to return—simply return. He will do the rest:

> I will heal their apostasy;
> I will freely love them. (Hos 14:4)

In the end, after the ordeal of their symbolic, incarnational marriage, after cycle upon cycle of disobedience and judgment, we are left standing with God's people (and with Gomer) exhausted before the Lord of hesed. We realize that we too are incapable of innocence. We are left before the One who nonetheless is kind to the ungrateful and the wicked (Lk 6:35).

It is all there in Hosea: stubborn disbelief and disobedience on the part of the people, and even more stubborn hesed on the part of God, who will not let his people go. As an expression of his lovingkindness he allows the people to experience the consequences of their sin, as he promised Moses in Exodus 34:7. It is a prophetic picture of the fragileness of human hesed and the enduring nature of the hesed of God.

Perhaps there is a Gomer in your life. Maybe you are a Gomer in someone else's life. Either way, the question is, How do we deal with unlovable people? (Even when that person is yourself.) We will see that Jesus, in Luke 6:35, says that God is kind to such unlovable, ungrateful, and even wicked people.

Soon after that passage in Luke we meet another Gomer, although we don't know her name. She interrupts a party at Simon the Pharisee's house in Luke 7:36-50. She is like Gomer in every way but one:

she has come to understand God's hesed. Her tears fall on Jesus' feet, and she impetuously wipes them dry with her hair. Somewhere, probably from the preaching of John the Baptist, she has heard the good news: a kingdom is here where unlovable people don't get what they deserve.

She experiences from Jesus himself how God reacts to the Gomers of this world. In response she *reciprocates* with her tears and tenderly wiping his feet in kindness. This is how the God of hesed treats every Gomer, and how they and we should respond to a kindness that is so relentlessly offered to us.

PART THREE

HESED FINALLY DEFINED

HESED AND TRUTH

13

Astronomers use a concept called averted vision to see very dim stars. When you examine the lengthy lists of star names, off to the side in parentheses you will occasionally see "AV." This means that particular star can be seen only by not looking directly at it. The central focus of the retina in the back of the eye is not as sensitive to light as the surrounding areas. So in order to see dimmer stars you look just beside them to engage the more light-sensitive parts of the back of the eye. You deliberately avert your vision to see what was already there yet was not seeable.

When we come to the New Testament, owing to the fact that we no longer have before us the Hebrew language, we must learn to "see" the word *hesed* by looking at it in a different way. Certainly hesed is there on every page of the New Testament, but seeing it without the presence of the actual Hebrew word requires some intensified listening.

We recognize hesed in the New Testament when we encounter the same characteristics we learned from listening to it in the Hebrew Bible. We recognize principles such as reciprocity and resonance, various phrases like "grace and truth," and a confidence in the character of God that allows someone to ask for what they do not deserve. In two rare incidents we actually hear the word from Jesus' lips.

One of the first clues to understanding the Hebrew concept of hesed in the Greek New Testament is found in the Septuagint, the ancient Greek translation of the Hebrew Bible. How did those ancient translators translate the word *hesed*? What Greek word did they choose? The answer in the vast majority of cases (almost two hundred times!) is a form of the word *eleos*, or "mercy." The word *charis* or "grace" is used only twice. The word for "righteousness" (*dikaiosunē*) is used five times. Once the word normally translated "hope" (*elpis*) is used. In total, a range of about seven words (including various forms) were employed by the translators of the Septuagint in rendering the Hebrew word *hesed*. Clearly, when they thought of *hesed*, the word that came to mind most often was *mercy*.

As we seek to understand the intersection of the world of *hesed* with the life of Jesus, we will see that it provides a significant piece of the puzzle that is his life. Hesed occupies a significant part of his teaching. It is expressed in virtually every one of his miracles. In one remarkable passage, Jesus even gives us his own definition of the word.

JOHN'S GOSPEL OF HESED

"The Word became flesh and dwelt among us. We observed his glory, the glory as the one and only Son from the Father, full of grace and truth" (Jn 1:14).

Our best sources tell us that John was ninety to one hundred years old when he wrote his elegant Gospel. Behind his words are decades of ministry, of constantly turning over in his youthful imagination who Jesus is and what he means. In the fourth Gospel, if you listen closely, you hear the echoes of sermons ("this is the verdict . . ."); you see numerous scenes of Jesus engaging at length with one single person, as a pastor would do. And being Jewish, John uses a lot of Hebrew words—only he writes in Greek.

The opening phrase of the Gospel, "In the beginning" (a phrase which also closes the first paragraph), is in fact a translation of the Hebrew title of the book of Genesis, *Bereshith*. But John does not simply use Hebrew words; he engages with the richness of their meaning. He is not simply implying *bereshith* by using the Greek *en arche*; he delves into the mystery that Jesus himself was from the beginning.

John is often misunderstood in his use of the Greek word *logos*, or "word." Because *logos* has certain philosophical connotations connected with the philosopher Heraclitus, who was an ancient resident of Ephesus, many assume that John has Greek philosophy in mind and is trying to connect with his Hellenistic readers. But though he writes in Greek, he thinks in Hebrew. Behind the Greek term *logos* is the Hebrew word *debar*. A simple overview of John's first chapter makes this clear. In the Hebrew Bible God creates through his word. Again and again in John 1, Jesus is revealed as precisely the one through whom God created everything (see Gen 1:3; Ps 33:6; 107:20; 147:18; 148:8; compare Col 1:16; Heb 1:2).

When it comes to the world of *hesed*, John begins his Gospel with a Greek translation of the most common phrase in the Hebrew Bible that incorporates the word *hesed*. When a Hebrew word or phrase makes it into the New Testament it is referred to as a "Hebraism." By far the most frequently used phrase in the Hebrew Scriptures connected to the word *hesed* is *hesed va emet*, which can be translated "grace and truth."

For example:

- "Blessed be the LORD, the God of my master Abraham, who has not withheld his *hesed va emet* from my master." (Gen 24:27)

- "If you don't report our mission, we will show *hesed va emet* to you." (Josh 2:14)

- "Now, may the LORD show *hesed va emet* to you." (2 Sam 2:6)

- "Your *hesed va emet* will always guard me." (Ps 40:11)

- "*Hesed va emet* go before you." (Ps 89:14)

We have already seen that the most significant occurrence of this phrase is found in Exodus 34:6. In that definitive moment, God describes himself as "abounding in *hesed va emet*," full of grace and truth. In his self-definition, in his explanation of his identity to Moses, God reveals that in him hesed and truth have come together in an overwhelming abundance.

When John sets himself to the task of describing Jesus in his prologue, he does not simply borrow the phrase "grace and truth," but he incorporates the same notion of fullness. Jesus is "full of grace and truth," he writes (Jn 1:14). It is a not-so-subtle hint to the divinity of Jesus, to his oneness with the Father.

THE MISUNDERSTOOD MESSIAH

Remember, when John uses a Hebraism like "grace and truth" he is going to fully integrate its context and meaning from the Hebrew Scriptures. He is not simply borrowing, he is integrating. One of the central themes from Exodus that is tied to God's character comes full-blown into John's picture of Jesus with the phrase *hesed va emet*: the fact that God is fundamentally misunderstood. Again and again the Israelites failed to grasp the true character of the One who is full of *hesed va emet*. They suspected that he had lured them into the wilderness only to kill them all. They refused the provision of the Promised Land. "Why do they despise me?" God responded to Moses. Which is to say, "How could they fail to understand that I love them as a father?" These are the words of one whose lovingkindness was constantly misunderstood and rejected.

This is *precisely* John's understanding of Jesus, the One who was also full of grace and truth. It is the central theme of his portrait of Jesus:

- "The light shines in the darkness, and the darkness did not comprehend it." (Jn 1:5 NKJV)

- "He was in the world, and the world was created through him, and yet the world did not recognize him." (Jn 1:10)

- "He came to his own, and his own people did not receive him." (Jn 1:11)

Every significant statement made by Jesus in the Gospel of John is misunderstood. When Jesus speaks to Nicodemus of the new birth, the old Pharisee can only stammer about the impossibility of reentering the birth canal. When he offers the Samaritan woman living water, all she sees is the fact that Jesus has no bucket at hand.[1]

Jesus is the misunderstood Messiah, who, like his Father, the God of Exodus 34 with whom he is one (Jn 10:30), chooses nevertheless to act out of the hesed and truth of which he is full to overflowing. He inaugurates the new covenant, where a new righteousness is granted and the law that had been written on stone is written on our hearts. He will not condemn. He will not judge. He will love, and because of the nature of his grace and truth, he will die. Jesus will make perfect provision on behalf of the One who swore to Moses that he would not leave the guilty unpunished. Though we have no right to expect anything from Jesus, he will nonetheless give us everything precisely because, like his Father, he is full of grace and truth.

When we become preoccupied with listening to what the Scriptures say about *hesed*—moreover, as we become serious about what it costs to "do" hesed—we will inevitably experience what Jesus experienced; we too will be misunderstood. In a world that operates by concepts like "You can't get something for nothing," the bearers of the good news are bound to be misunderstood when they proclaim, "God delights in giving you everything for nothing!" Though you have a right to expect nothing from him, he gives you everything.

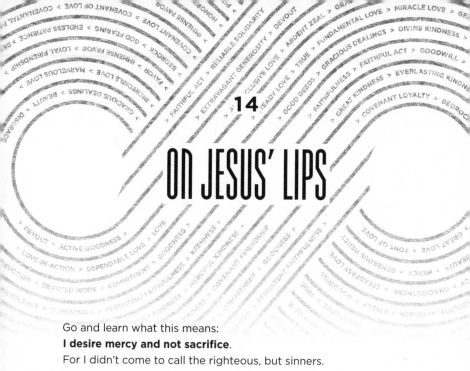

14

ON JESUS' LIPS

Go and learn what this means:
I desire mercy and not sacrifice.
For I didn't come to call the righteous, but sinners.

MATTHEW 9:13

If you had known what this means,
I desire mercy and not sacrifice,
you would not have condemned the innocent.

MATTHEW 12:7

We scan and strain, we listen for echoes of our special word, we analyze Hebraisms, all the while longing to simply hear it from his lips. That word, our word: *hesed*. Can any word be true until Jesus speaks it? He will define it. He will "parableize" concerning it. But Jesus, just let us hear you say it! And say it he does, in two precious passages in Matthew's Gospel.[1]

There are two separate scenes, in Matthew 9 and 12. Both incidents involve conflict with the Pharisees. The settings are different. The first takes place in Matthew's house, shortly after he responds to Jesus' call to follow him. The second incident takes place in an unspecified grain field, presumably located outside one of the towns where Jesus has been preaching in the synagogue. In both cases, Matthew leaves us in the dark as to the tone of Jesus' voice. There is no reference to his becoming impatient or irritated, although it is safe to assume a certain degree of tension in the air.

In Matthew 9:9, in the midst of a collection of miracle stories, Matthew tells the story of the miracle of Jesus reaching out to him. He and his fellow tax collectors would have been looked on as traitors for collaborating with the Romans.

We have a couple of hints at what must have been the norm in regards to the corruption of tax collectors in general. First, in Luke 3:12-13 some tax collectors come to John the Baptist with the question, "Teacher, what should we do?" John's response is that they should not collect any more taxes than they have been authorized to collect. Second, Luke 19 describes the conversion of Zacchaeus, who essentially confesses that he has been extorting money from the people. His declaration in Luke 19:8 that he will repay four times the amount he has stolen is itself a confession that he is a thief (see Ex 22:1-4).

Matthew was considered a corrupt outsider. It is safe to say he would have had no expectation whatsoever that someone like Jesus would reach out to him. Luke's Gospel tells us that in response to Jesus' extravagant invitation, Matthew gave a "grand banquet" (Lk 5:29). Naturally, Matthew invited his friends, who no doubt were just as corrupt and confused as Matthew was.

As best we can glean from the ancient sources, there were two schools of Pharisees in Jesus' time. Although they would eventually become the majority, at that time the followers of Hillel were the least influential group. Joseph of Arimathea and Nicodemus were in all likelihood followers of Hillel. Paul's teacher, Gamaliel, was the grandson of Hillel. Hillel was a lover of Gentiles and taught that the proper way to study the Torah was to gather people in. In Jesus' day he was the principal proponent of hesed.

The group that seems to follow Jesus about, scrutinizing his every move, were likely the followers of Shammai. By contrast to Hillel, Shammai was looked on as being severe and exacting. His followers were known to have resorted to violence to enforce Shammai's teaching. Shammai taught that when God created the Gentiles he made a mistake. He said the proper way to study the Torah was to push everyone else away. Some believe this is where the term *Pharisee*, meaning the "separated ones," originated.

In Matthew 9:11 the Shammanite Pharisees ask Jesus' disciples what he is doing sharing meal fellowship with tax collectors and sinners. It is likely a genuine question. There doesn't seem to be any sign of duplicity. They are not trying to trap Jesus with the question, as they will do later in Jerusalem.

In response, Jesus acknowledges that Matthew and his friends indeed are "sick." He is the doctor who has come to heal what's wrong with them (Mt 9:12). In Jesus' mind it is just that simple. The implication is that the Pharisees do not recognize that they too are ill and need Jesus' healing. In time, however, many of them will realize that they do need him.

Jesus then says, very rabbinically, "Go and learn what this means" (Mt 9:13). Again, his words are not necessarily confrontational. If the Pharisees are in time able to understand the passage Jesus quotes from Hosea 6:6, they will indeed realize why Jesus is showing kindness to a group of people who are thought to be unworthy of God's mercy.

Then, at last, Jesus says it: "I desire *hesed* and not sacrifice." That line appears in one of the laments in Hosea. Hosea 6:4 opens with the sad word that the hesed of God's people is fragile and vanishes like the morning mist. To a people who have been preoccupied with complex religious observance and the temple cult, Hosea counters that what God has desired all along is simple lovingkindness. He would rather his people be kind than offer a sacrifice. In verse 6, which seems to be in parallel poetic structure, the "knowledge of God" is paralleled with hesed. It is a passage the followers of Shammai would have known by heart, only it was not *in* their hearts but only in their heads. Jesus hopes that if they learn what this Scripture really means, then the radical reversal, the new reality he has come to proclaim, will become clear to them.

In the second story, in Matthew 12:1-8, Jesus and his disciples are picking heads of raw grain on the Sabbath, probably rubbing them between their hands to separate the seeds from the husks. According to the Torah they are perfectly within their rights (see Deut 23:25). They are allowed by law to gather grain from the corners of the field, as long as they do not use a metal tool, since that would be harvesting.

But on top of the Torah the Pharisees have heaped the oral law. They claim that God gave it to Moses on Mount Sinai during the forty days he lingered there. When Moses came down from the mountain he entrusted the Ten Commandments to the priests, who placed them in the ark of the covenant. According to the Pharisees, Moses then entrusted the oral law to the elders, of whom they claim to be the direct descendants. (Hence their assertion, "We're Moses's disciples"; Jn 9:28.)

The Pharisees are unable to see a group of hungry men, tired from ministry. They see only a violation of their oral law. Again, in Jesus' mind the solution is that they go to the Scriptures, and again to Hosea 6:6. If they could only understand the heart of the God of hesed, they would not condemn innocent people who are only dealing with their hunger.

When we see Jesus engage the small clutches of Shammanite Pharisees, we must understand that he is coming up against an entire system that is broken and fragmented. The Romans appointed the high priests in Jesus' day. They kept the garments of the priests in their possession in the Antonia Fortress. The holy of holies was an empty room in Herod's magnificent temple. No one agreed on canon, resurrection, angels, heaven, and hell. The topic almost everyone seemed to agree on, however, was Sabbath. Although there were minor disagreements as to how it should be observed, virtually all Jewish people agreed on the significance of observing the Sabbath. It was their dearest point of orthodoxy.

In the conclusion of the second story, Matthew records one of the most provocative statements Jesus ever made: "The Son of Man is Lord of the Sabbath" (Mt 12:8). Essentially he is saying, "Take your dearest point of orthodoxy. Okay? *I am Lord over that!*" Matthew does not record the response of the Pharisees, although is not hard to imagine.[2]

According to these two stories it is safe to say that in Jesus' mind Hosea 6:6 provides an antidote, a solution, a means by which the Pharisees' hardheartedness might be healed, if only they will *shema* with all of their "muchness" (Deut 6:4-5). Their inability to perceive brokenness and hunger in the people around them is a direct result of the fact that they have not understood the heart of God as it is revealed in the words of the prophet Hosea. There it is made clear that knowing God means understanding that his deepest desire is for hesed.

Jesus left radical reversal in the wake of his ministry. Because of the hesed of God incarnate in Jesus, sinners are blessed, while those who hate hesed place themselves outside of God's lovingkindness. Jesus having meal fellowship with tax collectors and sinners was an act of hesed. If the Pharisees had understood the kindness of God, they would've made the disciples' hunger more important than the rigorous observance of their oral tradition regarding the Sabbath. In

Jesus' mind, the obvious solution for their hardheartedness is an understanding of Hosea 6:6. There is a cure for hypocrisy. It is hesed.

Phariseeism could be wiped out in our time if we could understand that God would rather have us love someone well than offer a sacrifice.

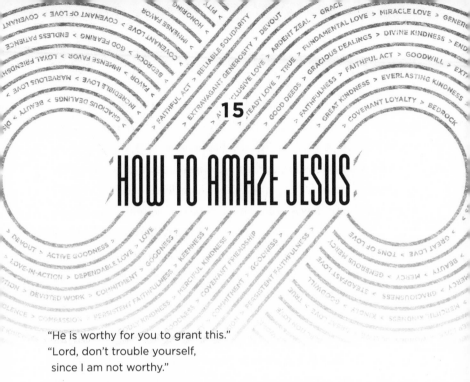

15

HOW TO AMAZE JESUS

"He is worthy for you to grant this."
"Lord, don't trouble yourself,
since I am not worthy."

LUKE 7:4, 6

The consistent testimony Luke heard from the eyewitnesses he interviewed while writing his Gospel was that they were all amazed. Some thirty years after they had seen and heard Jesus, they were still astonished by him. We believe this because in his Gospel Luke exhausts the language of amazement. Of the seven Greek words that can be translated "amazed" or "astonished" or "awed" or "astounded," Luke uses every single one of them. His is the only Gospel that does. What's more, he frequently uses two words for amazement in the same sentence (for example, Lk 5:26). The shepherds are amazed, as are Joseph and Mary. The people in Jesus' hometown of Nazareth are astonished, as are the residents of Capernaum, where Jesus relocated. Those who witness the miracles, who hear Jesus' synagogue sermons, were all of them amazed.

As Luke's narrative moves along, if you are really listening, you begin to wonder whether Jesus will ever be amazed. You have to wait seven long chapters to finally see it happen.

As the story opens Jesus returns to Capernaum, a large city on the northern shore of the Sea of Galilee, where Jesus had established a temporary home. It was primarily a fishing village, but archaeologists have uncovered so many large basalt millstones that they have begun to theorize that it was also a center of industry that produced them.

Upon entering the city, Jesus receives a message from a nameless Roman soldier. He is apparently a "God-fearer"—that is, he has made a preliminary commitment to Judaism. He keeps the three pillars of fasting, prayer, and giving to the poor but has yet to become a full proselyte. Beyond that, he has made an extravagant donation to the Jewish community of funds for a new synagogue. Its basalt foundations can still be seen in the excavations of Capernaum. In Judaism all of this means one thing: he is worthy. He's done all the right things and deserves any favor Jesus might do for him. That is, he has a right to expect something.

A further indication of the influence of Judaism on the soldier is the care he demonstrates for his sick slave. Romans were notoriously cruel slave masters, but clearly this centurion is a changed man. His heart and life have been shaped by the God of Exodus 34.

A delegation of elders from the community comes to Jesus with the request. They sum it all up in one phrase: "He is worthy for you to grant this" (Lk 7:4). That's it in a nutshell. The centurion prays correctly, fasts as he should, and gives to the poor. He has financed the new synagogue. He is worthy. The elders assume he has a right to expect Jesus to do something. This is not arrogance; it is simply the way the system works. Jesus silently responds by following them in the direction of the centurion's home, which was probably on the far eastern side of the city where a Roman military base has been excavated.

As Jesus and the elders come close to his home, they are met not by the soldier but by some of his friends. In Luke's account Jesus and the centurion never actually meet. The centurion has had some time to reconsider and has decided that Jesus does not need to come to his house after all. All he needs to do is simply say the word, and the slave will be healed. What follows is a fascinating speech from the Roman soldier on the theme of authority, how he has it and recognizes that Jesus does too. He understands the ability to command using a single word. But verse 6 says it all: "I do not deserve to have you come under my roof," the soldier says.

In my Bible I have those two statements circled with a line connecting them:

"This man deserves to have you do this" (Lk 7:4 NIV).

"I do not deserve . . ." (Lk 7:6 NIV).

Upon hearing this, Luke tells us, Jesus is "amazed" (Lk 7:9). He tells the Jewish crowd that he has yet to find this kind of faith in their community. But what exactly is the nature of the faith of the soldier? It is precisely his readiness to ask for what he acknowledges he does not deserve. At long last in Luke we see Jesus amazed by a simple soldier who understands that God is more loving than he has a right to expect.

To recognize all these details, to do word counts and draw circles and connect the ideas, may be interesting, but it falls short of truly listening to the text. If we are really paying attention and loving God by listening to his Word, we should stop and ask, Why? Why was Jesus amazed? What amazed him? Who amazed him?

The answer is obvious. The soldier's response amazed Jesus. His acknowledgment that, though he had done everything right, he was still undeserving amazed Jesus. But most of all, I believe what astounded the Lord was the fact that though the centurion confessed he was not worthy still he had the confidence and boldness to ask Jesus,

to do it anyway. Here is a pagan centurion who seems to intuit that
though he has no right to expect anything from Jesus, he can ask for
and expect to receive everything. He understands something his
Jewish neighbors have yet to figure out. The way you respond to the
God of Exodus 34, the God of hesed, is to boldly ask him for what you
do not deserve and then to stand by and confidently wait for him to
be amazed.

The context of the story of the centurion in Luke 7 is one of tension,
tension between the old orthodoxy and the new reality. The elders
expect Jesus to honor their request because of the obedience and generosity of the Roman soldier. The soldier, on the other hand, seems to
understand that what he has done does not entitle him to Jesus' favor.
He nevertheless seems to understand that because of the lovingkindness of the God of hesed, he can ask for what he does not deserve.
Though it is rightly listed as one of the miracle stories of Jesus, the
point of the story is not the healing of the servant. The highlight of the
story is the amazement of Jesus.

Of all the ways hesed might possibly come to life in us, of all the
myriad ways it might be applied, this passage provides the best example, in my opinion. The person who understands the lovingkindness of God is always ready to persistently seek, ask, and knock
on the door that opens up to a world they have done nothing to deserve. As we come to understand God's hesed we will have a growing
confidence that he is delighted to give us his blessings. Like the centurion, our attitude will become "Just say the word . . ."

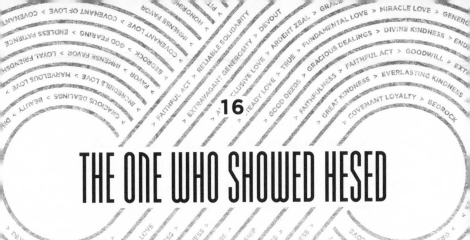

16

THE ONE WHO SHOWED HESED

"Which of these three do you think proved to be a neighbor
to the man who fell into the hands of the robbers?"

"The one who showed mercy to him," he said.

Then Jesus told him, "Go and do the same."

LUKE 10:36-37

If hesed is central to Jesus' heart and mind, you would expect it to
show up in his teaching, as in fact it does. In eight of the thirty parables, hesed is the central theme. Even in the parables that don't deal
specifically with hesed, it nonetheless appears. The unforgiving
servant in Matthew 18 is guilty because he fails to show hesed. The
implication in the parable of the rich man and Lazarus is that the unnamed wealthy man is guilty partially because he failed to show
mercy (Lk 19:31).

Jesus' parables function in two ways. First, he tells his brief stories
in such a way that individual hearers will identify with one or another of the characters. Who you identify with tells a lot about who
you are. Do you stand with those who do hesed or not? Secondly,

Jesus' parables are open ended. They are intended to leave you not necessarily with an answer, but with a better question. They are invitations to *shema*, to listen with everything you are. ("He who has ears, *shema*!" Jesus often says.) One of the best examples of this lack of closure is the parable of the good Samaritan.

Luke likes to show us parables at work. By this I mean he frequently gives us the setting and the composition of the crowd, and after the story is told he sometimes shows us its effects. In Luke 10:25-37 Jesus tells the story of the good Samaritan. We know the story so well we may mistakenly think we have squeezed it dry. But that is not the way of Jesus' parables.

We know from Luke 9:51 that the great central section of the Gospel, known as the travel narrative, has begun. This means Jesus is on his way to Jerusalem for the last time. The cross is waiting for him there. It casts a shadow over all ten chapters of the great central section (9:51-19:41).

Luke gives us the setting of the story: a trick question asked by one of the scribes to test Jesus. (Once he arrives in Jerusalem these kinds of questions will become more frequent.) It is a flawed question: "What must I do to inherit eternal life?" (Lk 10:25). One of the innovations of Jesus' teaching is that it is not what we do that earns us eternal life. Jesus responds, "What is written in the law?" (Lk 10:26). This is a question the scribe could answer in his sleep. He responds with the second half of Jesus' favorite biblical passage, the Shema. It says we should love God with everything we are, all of our "muchness" (*me'od*). To Deuteronomy 6 the scribe adds from Leviticus 19:18 "love your neighbor as yourself."

It might have all ended then and there. A question asked and correctly answered. "Do this and you will live," Jesus responds to the initial question about eternal life (Lk 10:28). But, says Luke, the scribe wants to justify himself. He wants some sort of acknowledgment from

Jesus that he is righteous and deserves eternal life. So he counters in verse 29 with the question, "And who is my neighbor?"

Notice that Jesus gives absolutely no introduction, no explanation. He simply launches into a story that takes fifty-seven seconds to tell. It is consistent with geography. The steep road from Jerusalem down to Jericho, "the city of the priests," was a dangerous route. The presence of a priest and Levite makes sense. Many who labored in the temple chose to live in Jericho. The unfortunate person who falls into the hands of "men of violence" is neither Jew nor Gentile. He is simply wounded and in need. That is all we need to know about him.

Both the priest and the Levite seem to be going home, downhill, back from their time of service at the temple. When the crowd hears how they both step aside from the bloody wounded man to avoid ceremonial uncleanness, no one bats an eye. Of course, this is what we expect them to do. According to the old orthodoxy, ritual purity is high on the list of the things we do to inherit eternal life. But the Hebrew Scriptures speak of other things, specifically having to do with hesed.

We don't hear a murmur from the crowd until the Samaritan is mentioned. He would have elicited a few derisive snorts. And yet he is the one who "takes pity"—that is, he is the one who does hesed. He bandages, pours wine and oil, and loads the wounded man on his own donkey. He takes him to the inn, presumably in Jericho. While they are there he cares for him, pays the bill for them both (two coins), and promises to pay any extra expenses the wounded man may incur.

In Jesus' parables expressions of hesed tend to have this over-the-top character. The father of the prodigal son sprints out with a ring and robe and shoes. He puts on an extravagant feast with orchestrated music. That is the nature of hesed. Manna, quail, living water, and a land flowing with milk and honey; protection, provision, and presence.

Characteristically, Jesus leaves the scribe not with an answer but with a question: Who was the neighbor to the wounded man that Leviticus 19 says he should love?

I imagine the scribe looking down at the ground as he answers, avoiding the use of the word *Samaritan*. His circumlocution says it all: "The one who showed mercy" (i.e., did hesed).

Jesus responds, "Go and do the same" (Lk 10:37). It is the answer to the first flawed question from verse 25, "What must I do?" In the Hebrew mind hesed is always something you do. It is a verb. It is loading wounded people on donkeys, running to greet runaway children, forgiving enormous debts, paying someone who worked an hour as much as the ones who worked all day, giving a party to those who can't pay you back. It is a resonant response to the overwhelming kindness of the God of Exodus 34, who is full of hesed. Only Luke tells the parables of the good Samaritan and the prodigal son. And only Luke provides us with Jesus' magnificent definition of hesed.

In Luke 6 Jesus tells his followers that they should love their enemies; they should bless those who curse them and offer the other cheek to someone who strikes them. If someone takes your sweater, says Jesus, give them your shirt too. It is the cost of embracing the new reality over the old orthodoxy. If you are fully engaged and you listen to the text in Luke, you will feel the anxiety of his first disciples and perhaps even the outrage of the scribes and Pharisees.

Then comes the most remarkable thing Jesus ever said. It is the best encouragement he can think of in helping us to love our enemies. We do so, according to Jesus, because God loves *his* enemies. We will be his sons and daughters if we can find it in our redeemed souls to love as he does. And then come these magnificent, shocking, unbelievable words describing the hesed of the Most High: "He is kind to the ungrateful and wicked" (Lk 6:35). Hesed is almost always an extravagant expression of kindness, forgiveness, and love. It is something you do. It is the only appropriate response to the One who has shown his kindness to us, the "ungrateful and evil."

Those parting words, "go and do the same," are spoken to you and me every bit as much as they were to the scribe.

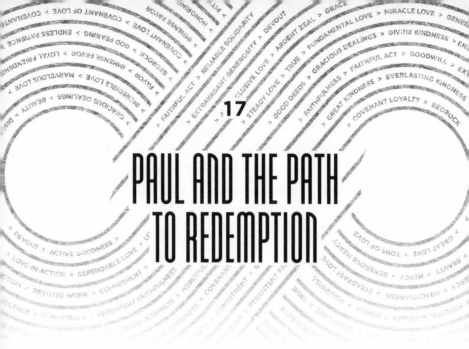

17

PAUL AND THE PATH TO REDEMPTION

Or do you despise the riches of his kindness, restraint, and patience, not recognizing that God's kindness is intended to lead you to repentance?

ROMANS 2:4

What we thought would be a routine procedure dragged out to three days in the hospital. The surgeon was amazingly kind, as were the nurses who meticulously cared for us. On the second day, when I began to realize that we might have a longer stay ahead, I went down to the store for some "possibles" we would need. When I filed into the checkout line, there was a woman ahead of me with as many items in her hands as I had. She smiled and said, "Why don't you go ahead of me." Little did she know the minefield she had just stepped into.

"Oh, I couldn't do that," I said. "My mother didn't raise me to break in line, and what's more I was always taught to let girls go first," I said jokingly, but also kind of serious.

She patiently smiled, but insisted again that I go ahead: "I have some questions, and I don't want you to have to wait on me."

"But I would be glad to wait," I said, still trying to be considerate, kind, my mother's son, and so on.

Then she said something that suddenly brought tears to my eyes. There are tears in my eyes at this moment as I write these words, though I'm not sure I completely understand why.

"Why won't you let me be kind to you?" she said.

Why wouldn't I? In my mind, apparently kindness counted only when I did it for someone else. In that small encounter I learned a new lesson. If you truly love hesed as Micah 6:8 says, you should love having it shown to you as much as showing it to others. As Paul says, it's a pathway, and it can be traveled in more than one way.

Perhaps something like this is in view when Paul asks why we sometimes despise the riches of God's kindness. Why would we question him in the garden? Why would we refuse to enter the Promised Land? Why would we say no to his extravagant offer of loving us through his Son? His kindness is a path that leads us to repentance, that leads us to Jesus.

Paul is not the systematic theologian he is sometimes made out to be. He is a church-planting pastor, overpowered by the grace and mercy of God. Though Paul had been a persecutor of the church, ungrateful, even wicked, Jesus forgave him and enlisted him to become one of its most influential apostles. Paul had become a sure recipient of hesed, and he remained amazed by it for the rest of his life. He offers encouragement and deals with problems in his letters. And like the other New Testament writers, he thinks in Hebrew and writes in Greek. We do not consult the letters of Paul like a theological answer book. Rather, we go to Paul to find the answers to problems and conflicts in the church and in our lives. That was the original purpose of his writing. He was writing to encourage the young church as it faced impossible obstacles. If he has a theology (and certainly he does), it is what William Lane calls a "task theology."

To be honest, hesed as we have sought to define it is not prevalent in the writings of Paul. Twice he quotes Old Testament passages but frustratingly stops just before the word *hesed* appears (Rom 15:9, 10). Scholars cannot even agree on what Greek word he used when he was talking about hesed. Some say *agape* (love), while others argue for *charis* (grace). But understanding hesed is not a matter of settling on one single term. Its semantic range is simply too vast. Grace, mercy, and love are central to Paul's understanding of God's free offer of forgiveness. In his writings, they are less technical theological terms and far more about describing the heart of God.

There is another term Paul uses that often describes the character of God and belongs in the world of hesed. It is the Greek word *chrēstotēs*, usually translated "kindness" (see Rom 2:4; 2 Cor 6:6; Gal 5:22; Col 3:12; Titus 3:4).[1] We have seen that this idea falls close to the center of the semantic range of *hesed*. The word most often appears in the midst of the "chain sayings" Paul (and Peter) was so fond of. In Ephesians 2:7 Paul speaks about the immeasurable riches of God's grace being displayed through his kindness (*chrēstotēs*) to us in Christ Jesus. But two passages in Romans speak most clearly of God's hesed as Paul seems to understand it.

We are not certain when the church in Rome was founded. There is no attribution to a single apostle. When Paul communicates to the believers in Rome, it is clear they have already been gathering for some time, perhaps as early as AD 40. When he arrives in the city he is greeted by a strong group of the followers of Jesus from an apparently well-established church that demonstrates remarkable hospitality (Acts 28:13-15). In his letter to the Romans, Paul comments that they are known all over the world (Rom 1:8). But a crisis overshadows the church.

Suetonius wrote about a riot in the city in AD 49 over someone he referred to as Chrestus. It is a slave name that means "good one." Historians agree that it is, in fact, a garbled form of the name Christos. As a result of the disturbance, Emperor Claudius ordered that all the Jews be banished from the city. This would include Jewish Christians as well. As a result the Roman church was divided. The Jews were sent away, while the Gentile believers remained behind.

From the beginning Jesus had been worshiped in Hebrew as Messiah; then as the remaining Gentiles filled the leadership vacuum he was celebrated in Greek as Kurios, or Lord. In AD 54 Claudius died, and as was the custom his edicts were canceled. The Jews returned to Rome (see Acts 18:2), and tension in the church began to rise. Before the expulsion, leadership was primarily Jewish. In the gap caused by the edict, Gentiles had taken up leadership. They had been shaping the church for five years. This is the central problem Paul is dealing with in the letter to the Romans. There are leadership struggles and disagreements in the body as to who Jesus is and how he should be celebrated. Believers are judging one another and factions are forming.

In his letter Paul gives two reasons for writing. First, he has been trying to come to them but has been prevented thus far (Rom 1:10, 13). Second, he wants to encourage them and be encouraged by them (Rom 1:12). Paul begins in chapter 1 with a discussion of sin. He goes on to encourage the church to not get caught up in the sins of paganism and to also avoid the sin of passing judgment on those who do.

The context of Paul's allusion to hesed in Romans 2:4 is the previous discussion of sin in the Gentile world. In the opening verses of chapter 2 he is insisting the church, given the pagan environment, must also keep from the sin of being judgmental, for when they judge others they are really judging themselves. In that context he makes an extraordinary statement that relates to the hesed character of God:

"Or do you despise the riches of his kindness, restraint, and patience, not recognizing that God's kindness [*chrēstotēs*] is intended to lead you to repentance?"

The best motivator to keep the Roman Christians, both Jew and Gentile, from becoming mired in their sinful pagan surroundings, and also to keep them from judging each other in the process, is to remember the revelation of God's character that goes all the way back to Exodus 34. He is a God of *hesed*. It is not fear that drives us to him, but rather his unexpected and extraordinary kindness that provides a pathway along which we are drawn to him.

PART FOUR

AN INSTINCT FOR HESED

18

HERE, RABBI, TAKE MY SEAT

It's night at the Philadelphia airport. I'm boarding the rental car shuttle in the rain. Despite the late hour, the bus is packed, and I'm the last person to board. Just behind me, standing in the rain, is an Orthodox rabbi. He has ear-locks, and I can see the tzitzit, the fringes of the corner of his prayer shawl, hanging beneath his black coat. His gray beard is long. He has an ancient, wizened, and remarkably handsome face.

As I take my seat it occurs to me that I should jump off the bus and invite him to have my place. After all, I can grab the next bus. I think to myself, *I will whisper, "Hesed, my brother," as we change places. (Let's see, what would that be in Hebrew . . .)* What a wonderful moment that could be. *Let's make a memory*, I say to myself, *and then I'll . . .*

At that moment the door of the shuttle bus closed. I missed my chance to reach out to the rabbi, still standing in the rain. My intentions were good, but my timing was miserable. I'd wasted precious seconds deciding how to play out the details of the scenario in my mind. I missed the chance to "do hesed." What should've been an instinct, an immediate, intuitive response, was instead a self-centered, self-serving mental exercise.

Dejected and deeply disappointed in myself, I committed at that moment to develop an instinct to do hesed. Then and there I asked the Lord of lovingkindness to transform my heart, to shape it like his heart.

Developing an instinct to do hesed became the fundamental tenet of Judaism after the destruction of the temple in AD 70. If we are genuinely committed to this journey of understanding all that hesed means, it might be good to look at a group of men and women who have been on this journey for over three thousand years.

19

HESED IN POST-AD 70 JUDAISM

No discussion of the word *hesed* would be complete without an overview of how it is applied in the world of Judaism, the world where this unique concept was born and the world that for thousands of years has struggled to apply the practice of hesed to everyday life in the midst of often unspeakably hostile surroundings. As you might expect, the literature is vast, and these few pages will provide only the briefest introduction.

Before the destruction of the temple by the Romans in AD 70, hesed's role in Judaism is illustrated pretty much by the same attitudes we see in the Gospels and Acts. Amid a fragmented Judaism, hesed was held by some like Hillel and his followers as central, as the key to understanding the character of God and what he expects from his children. On the other side of the spectrum were teachers like Shammai and his larger, more influential following. Shammai was known to be severe in his opinions by and large. Hesed was not integral to his system of thought; rather, a rigid personal righteousness was central. Shammai perceived the character of God in much the same light. He believed that the Lord disdained Gentiles. Shammai's school taught that God might "set aside" a person's sins on judgment day as long as they maintained

a strict level of legal observance and personal righteousness, while
Hillel taught that the Lord would "wash our sins away." Between the
extremes of those two schools we can imagine all sorts of shades of gray.

Everything would radically change on the ninth of Av (August 10)
in AD 70 when Titus burned Herod's magnificent temple to the ground.
What was already a fragmented faith seemed by all appearances to be
coming to a smoldering end.

The Talmud tells the fascinating story of the moment when, as the
smoke was still rising from the ruins of Jerusalem, Judaism was born
anew, re-visioned by a follower of Hillel named Yohanan ben Zakkai.
I alluded to this story earlier; here is the passage in full:

> Once Rabbi Yochanan ben Zakkai was leaving Jerusalem. Rabbi
> Yehoshua was following behind him and saw the ruins of the
> Temple. Rabbi Yehoshua said: Woe to us for this! The place
> where atonement was obtained for Israel's sins is in ruins. He
> replied: My son, let this not sadden you. We have another form
> of atonement which is equal to this. And what is it? Gemiluth
> hesed [the practice of hesed] as it is said; 'For I desire hesed and
> not sacrifice.' Hos. 6:6.[1]

What might have been a violent end of Judaism was in fact its re-
birth. Until the destruction of the temple, Shammai's school had represented the center of power. Then Hillel's followers took leadership
of the thought life of Israel. They became the shapers of the Judaism
we know today. As happens so often in the Scriptures, it was precisely
suffering that God used to reshape his people. Where there had been
division and fragmentation there was now a new righteousness and
a new lens through which to look at the world: hesed.

Hesed is not simply a Hebrew word—it is a Hebrew ideal. Befitting
the more verbal Hebrew mind, it is always looked on as something

you do. You come to understand hesed not by defining it but by doing it. Acts of hesed extend God's image out into the world.

Ethan the Ezrahite had sung, "I will sing about the LORD's *hesed* forever" (Ps 89:1). This idea became central in rabbinic discussions for centuries to come. In one of his lectures, Rabbi Yerucham Levovitz says, "*Hesed* is not only the most important theme of the Torah, it is the theme of everything; all of Torah and of Creation flows from the value of hesed."[2] *Hesed* is at the heart of the contemporary Jewish search for meaning. Here are some of the things the Talmud has to say about hesed:

- "He who occupies himself with Torah study alone without doing acts of *hesed* is as if he had no G-d." (Avodah Zarah 17b)

- "Acts of *hesed* rescue a man from the clutches of his evil desires." (Avodah Zarah 5b)

- "The world stands on three things; Torah, service of G-d and acts of *hesed*." (Pirkei Avos 1:2)

- "Acts of *hesed* are greater than righteousness [*tzedakah*]." (Sukkot 49b; referencing Hosea 10:12)

Across the spectrum of modern Judaism, the doing of hesed remains absolutely central. Some sects focus almost exclusively on acts of kindness toward other Jews, while others have taken on social activism as an expression of their commitment to doing hesed. To begin to understand hesed in modern Jewish observance, two important terms provide a good start: *gemilut hesed* and *tikkun olam*.

Both of these terms (like *rabbi* and *synagogue*) are postbiblical. *Gemilut hesed*, or "the practice of hesed," refers to the many different ways hesed can be done. The second phrase describes the healing effect doing hesed has on the culture and the world: *tikkun olam*, "repairing the world." Simply put, the repairing of the world is accomplished through acts of *hesed*.

20

GEMILUT HESED AND TIKKUN OLAM

"The Torah begins and ends with hesed," says the Talmud (Sotah 14a). The first and final acts of God in the Pentateuch are both *gemilut hasidim*. In Genesis 3:21 he clothes the nakedness of Adam and Eve. Caring for the poor is one of the foundational acts of hesed. Then in Deuteronomy 34:6 God buries Moses. Caring for the dead is referred to as *hesed shel emet*, "the truest act of kindness." Such care is highly regarded due to the fact that the deceased cannot give you any thanks. An act done in secret or without any regard for receiving payment of thanks is the pinnacle of the acts of hesed (see Mt 6:3; Lk 14:13).

Other paradigm acts of hesed are *bikkur cholim*, visiting the sick; *nichum aveilim*, comforting mourners; *hakhnasat orchim*, showing hospitality; and *hakhnasat kallah*, bringing in the bride.[1]

Tikkun olam, or "repairing the world," was a concept initially used in the second century in the Mishnah to protect women from frivolous divorce, but it resurfaced in Judaism in the 1950s. The phrase is based on the presupposition that the world is sick and broken. Whereas *gemilut hesed* implies that acts of kindness should be discreet, *tikkun olam* speaks of open engagement in social issues in the world, or social activism.[2]

In recent years there has been a movement to repair the notion of *tikkun olam*, as some more conservative rabbis believe that people are beginning to take upon themselves something that belongs only to God. Only he can fix this unfixable world. These rabbis have proposed a twenty-year moratorium on the term, claiming it has completely lost its original meaning.[3]

Some examples of *tikkun olam* are *hevra kaddisha*, funeral societies; Yad Sara, a group that loans medical equipment; and *enosh*, home-bound care for the elderly.[4]

To close this discussion very rabbinically, here is a parable that illustrates both *gemilut hesed* and *tikkun olam*. It is attributed to Rabbi Heim of Romshishok and is known as the parable of the spoons. (For just a moment, disengage your New Testament cosmology. This is not a story about heaven, it is an illustration of hesed.)

Once a man who was known for his acts of benevolence stood before a judge who would decide whether he would go to heaven or go to hell. The judge offered him a unique privilege, however. He told the man he could first visit heaven and hell and then choose between them. A chariot of fire then appeared and took the man off to a remote castle, floating upon a cloud. There he saw a great hall, filled with many tables. On each table were all sorts of delectable foods—the greatest feast imaginable. The man then heard the sound of sad chanting as many people entered the hall. The people came to the tables but could not eat, even though they were all emaciated and very hungry. On each person's left hand was tied a giant fork, and on their right was tied a giant spoon. They could not bend their elbows to bring any food to their mouths. An angel said to the man, "This is hell. Now go visit heaven."

The chariot of fire then took him to another castle floating upon a cloud. It looked just like the first. The great hall was also filled with many tables upon which were set all sorts of delectable foods. The man then heard the sound of happy chanting as many people entered the hall. The people came to the tables but they did not look emaciated. On each person's left hand was tied a giant fork, and on their right was tied a giant spoon. They could not bend their elbows to bring any food to their mouths. As the man watched, however, the people began to feed one another. Each person picked up food and carried it to his neighbor's mouth. The angel then said, "This is heaven. The people make it heaven since they have found a way to do gemilut hasidim."

The man then was brought before the judge again. "Have you decided to go to heaven or hell?" The man answered, "I choose hell. I will teach them the secret of creating heaven. This will be my last good deed."[5]

DO JUSTICE, LOVE MERCY, WALK HUMBLY

THE MONUMENTAL NATURE OF KINDNESS

Mankind, he has told each of you what is good
and what it is the LORD requires of you:
to act justly,
to love *hesed*,
and to walk humbly with your God.

MICAH 6:8

In Micah chapter 6, the Lord has brought Israel into the courtroom. He calls creation as his witness; he invites the people to testify as well, to plead their case against him. Through his many acts of mercy God has made it clear that he has acted in righteousness toward Israel. They are without defense; what they should have done is clear. It was not burnt offerings, rams, or streams of oil. He has told them what is good (*tov*). What he requires of them is

to act justly,
to love *hesed*,
and to walk humbly with your God.

God commands his people to *do* justly and to *love* hesed. We struggle with both. If it were simply a matter of doing justly *or* loving hesed, we might be able to come up with a formula, a set of rules to follow. But the two must function together. We can do justly only by loving hesed. The doing must flow from the loving. And the loving is a response, as love is always a response, to the God of Exodus 34, who is full of hesed and at the same time does not leave the guilty unpunished.

Bryan Stevenson has articulated this elegant unity between justice and mercy in his book *Just Mercy*. It is the finest synthesis of these two concepts I have ever read. In the context of working with those who were on death row, he discovered the secret of loving hesed. "Mercy," he writes, "is most transformative when it is directed at the undeserving."[1] And, "The power of just mercy is that it belongs to the undeserving."[2]

In Jesus of Nazareth, the embodiment of hesed, God was perfectly just and perfectly merciful. Through Jesus he fulfilled the promise to not leave the guilty unpunished by placing that punishment on Jesus in an act of pure and perfect hesed. Jesus did justice by loving hesed. He gave himself so that we might be conquered by the kindness of God, a kindness that leads us to repentance, that draws us to the cross. That moment in time makes doubting the lovingkindness of God impossible. It was the supreme moment of *tikkun olam*, of healing the world. As Frederick Buechner says, instead of being too good to be true, it's "too good not to be true."[3]

Hesed is all around us, in every moment, through acts of unselfish kindness. Some of them are extravagant, like Keshia Thomas saving the life of a man who had devoted his life to hating her. Some seem at first to be smaller, like Dinah reaching out and taking hold of my hand, but they are really no less extraordinary and life changing. Someone risks opening the door of his or her life to you.

In spite of yourself, you forgive an enemy who is not even seeking forgiveness. These luminous moments strike, and something deep within us resonates. Often we discover an unbidden tear in the eye when they do. This is what the world was created by. This is what we were created for.

The final challenge to you and me is to take whatever understanding we have in our heads of hesed and allow the Spirit to move it into our hearts. We must enter into the world of the word *hesed* and then take that world into our world, back to our families, to our churches and towns—to our enemies. The Scriptures are offering us an unimaginable opportunity to make Jesus believable and beautiful by offering everything (even our very lives) to those who have a right to expect nothing from us.

In the end it is not about some ancient, simple three-syllable word, it is about the *world* of hesed. It is about entering that world with an informed imagination and allowing that world to enter and transform us, as we develop an instinct to do kindness. Just like Moses, we must summon the courage to ask God to "teach us your ways" and "show us your glory."

As a final exercise of listening to the Word with all our muchness, most especially to this single untranslatable word *hesed*, let's integrate what we have seen from all the passages we've listened to into one summary statement, *one extended and fragmented definition of this inexpressible word.*

Hesed *is a defining characteristic of God. It is linked to his compassion and graciousness. It is expressed in his willingness to forgive wrongdoing and to take upon himself the sin, rebellion, and wrongdoing of his people. As an expression of his lovingkindness, God allows his people to experience the consequences of their sin, as he promised Moses in Exodus 34:7. Even this is an expression of his hesed.*

God can be approached boldly based on the confidence we have in this aspect of his revealed nature. He is amazingly kind and loving to his servants as well as to the ungrateful and wicked. He is delighted to show them kindness. Due to this, they marvel that no other god is like their God because of his hesed.

The scope of hesed is expanded in the context of worship. It is most often sung, as our hearts resonate sympathetically to the One who created us in his lovingkindness. However, when the reciprocal nature of hesed has been violated we are encouraged in the imprecatory psalms to offer feelings of anger and outrage, trusting in the hesed of the One who knows our hearts and will stand in solidarity with us and act on behalf of the poor. When we are facing despair we can take confidence in all God's former acts of lovingkindness. Hesed is a standard to which we can appeal. We understand that we can ask, beg, and expect to receive according to the standard of God's hesed.

In light of our inability to keep any of the covenants, God has graciously granted to us a new covenant, based solely on his faithfulness. That covenant came into effect and will be sustained by means of a person Jeremiah refers to as the "Righteous Branch." He is the incarnation of hesed, full of grace and truth.

AFTERWORD

My all-time favorite movie is an adaptation of a book by one of my favorite writers, Oliver Sacks. It's called *Awakenings*. It tells the true story of the author's experience as a young experimental physician who pioneered a new use for the drug L-DOPA to awaken patients who had been catatonic for decades. One by one they awoke, and sadly one by one most of them eventually fell back into a coma. It is an exceedingly powerful book and film.

In one scene, Sacks (magnificently played by the late Robin Williams) is weeping as he is forced to watch his patient's lapse back into oblivion. A nurse who has been his sole supporter in the hospital sits beside him as he weeps.

Sacks: "You told me I was a kind man. How kind is it to give life only to take it away again?"

Nurse: "It's given and taken away from all of us."

Sacks: "Why doesn't that comfort me?"

Nurse: "Because you are a kind man."[1]

It would be remiss of me not to mention the profound cost associated with doing hesed. It is vital that we realize that embracing hesed, developing an instinct for doing it in the world, inevitably means an encounter with woundedness, ours and the world's. Of course we are right to anticipate moments of profound joy and a deep sense of fulfillment. But to take lightly the cost that is involved would be a mistake. The backgrounds and the linguistics, the biblical passages, are all fascinating, but the doing of hesed is something else altogether. It is a costly enterprise, perhaps the most costly enterprise. It cost God everything.

That having been said, Micah 7:18 reminds us that God delights in doing hesed. And so should we. Hesed can shape our prayer life, our experience of worship, and most especially the posture we take as we engage with the world around us.

Finally, as the love of God defines us, so hesed provides the full meaning of that love. His lovingkindness radically redefines us—from fallen to beloved, from outcasts to daughters and sons. Hesed resonates in us because it is a part of who we were created to become; it represents what we are being transformed, recreated, reborn, redeemed to be. We must become *hasids*, not simply those who go about doing good works but men and women who are completely dependent on the hesed of God, conquered by his kindness, reborn to a life of unconditional love.

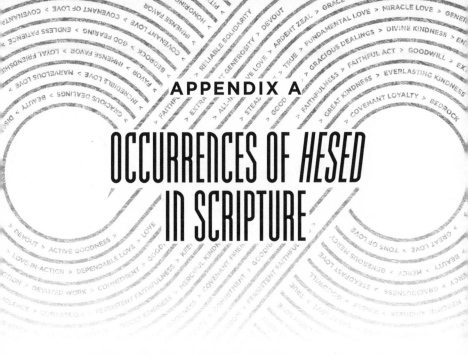

APPENDIX A

OCCURRENCES OF *HESED* IN SCRIPTURE

Quotations are from the Christian Standard Bible, with the words used to translate *hesed* in bold. Words in parentheses indicate the Septuagint's (LXX) Greek translation.

1. **Genesis 19:19.** Your servant has indeed found favor with you, and you have shown me **great kindness** by saving my life. But I can't run to the mountains; the disaster will overtake me, and I will die. (*eleos*)

2. **Genesis 20:13.** So when God had me wander from my father's house, I said to her: Show your **loyalty** to me wherever we go and say about me: "He's my brother." (*dikaiosunē*)

3. **Genesis 21:23.** As I have been **loyal** to you, so you will be **loyal** to me and to the country where you are a resident alien. (*dikaiosunē*)

4. **Genesis 24:12.** "Lord, God of my master Abraham," he prayed, "make this happen for me today, and show **kindness** to my master Abraham." (*eleos*)

5. **Genesis 24:14.** By this I will know that you have shown **kindness** to my master. (*eleos*)

6. **Genesis 24:27.** Blessed be the LORD, the God of my master Abraham, who has not withheld his **kindness** and faithfulness from my master. (*dikaiosunē*)

7. **Genesis 24:49.** Now, if you are going to show **kindness** and faithfulness to my master, tell me; if not, tell me, and I will go elsewhere. (*eleos*)

8. **Genesis 32:10.** I am unworthy of all the **kindness** and faithfulness you have shown your servant. (*dikaiosunē*)

9. **Genesis 39:21.** But the LORD was with Joseph and extended **kindness** to him. He granted him favor with the prison warden. (*eleos*)

10. **Genesis 40:14.** Please show **kindness** to me by mentioning me to Pharaoh, and get me out of this prison. (*eleos*)

11. **Genesis 47:29.** When the time approached for him to die, he called his son Joseph and said to him, "If I have found favor with you, put your hand under my thigh and promise me that you will deal with me in **kindness** and faithfulness." (*eleos*)

12. **Exodus 15:13.** With your **faithful love**, / you will lead the people / you have redeemed; / you will guide them to your holy dwelling / with your strength. (*dikaiosunē*)

13. **Exodus 20:6.** But showing **faithful love** to a thousand generations of those who love me and keep my commands. (*eleos*)

14. **Exodus 34:6.** The LORD passed in front of him and proclaimed: The LORD—the LORD is a compassionate and gracious God, slow to anger and abounding in **faithful love** and truth. (*eleos*)

15. **Exodus 34:7.** Maintaining **faithful love** to a thousand generations, forgiving iniquity, rebellion, and sin. But he will not leave the guilty unpunished, bringing the fathers' iniquity on the children and grandchildren to the third and fourth generation. (*eleos*)

16. **Leviticus 20:17.** If a man marries his sister, whether his father's daughter or his mother's daughter, and they have sexual relations, it is a **disgrace.**

17. **Numbers 14:18.** The LORD is slow to anger and abounding in **faithful love**, forgiving iniquity and rebellion. But he will not leave the guilty unpunished, bringing the consequences of the fathers' iniquity on the children to the third and fourth generation. (*eleos*)

18. **Numbers 14:19.** Please pardon the iniquity of this people, in keeping with the greatness of your **faithful love**, just as you have forgiven them from Egypt until now. (*eleos*)

19. **Deuteronomy 5:10.** But showing **faithful love** to a thousand generations of those who love me and keep my commands. (*eleos*)

20. **Deuteronomy 7:9.** Know that the LORD your God is God, the faithful God who keeps his gracious **covenant loyalty** for a thousand generations with those who love him and keep his commands. (*eleos*)

21. **Deuteronomy 7:12.** If you listen to and are careful to keep these ordinances, the LORD your God will keep his **covenant loyalty** with you, as he swore to your fathers. (*eleos*)

22. **Joshua 2:12.** Now please swear to me by the LORD that you will also show **kindness** to my father's family, because I showed **kindness** to you. Give me a sure sign. (*eleos*)

23. **Joshua 2:14.** The men answered her, "We will give our lives for yours. If you don't report our mission, we will show **kindness** and faithfulness to you when the LORD gives us the land." (*eleos*)

24. **Judges 1:24.** The spies saw a man coming out of the town and said to him, "Please show us how to get into town, and we will show you **kindness**." (*eleos*)

25. **Judges 8:35.** They did not show **kindness** to the house of Je-rubbaal (that is, Gideon) for all the good he had done for Israel. (*eleos*)

26. **Ruth 1:8.** May the LORD show **kindness** to you as you have shown to the dead and to me. (*eleos*)

27. **Ruth 2:20.** Then Naomi said to her daughter-in-law, "May the LORD bless him because he has not abandoned his **kindness** to the living or the dead." (*eleos*)

28. **Ruth 3:10.** Then he said, "May the LORD bless you, my daughter. You have shown more **kindness** now than before, because you have not pursued younger men, whether rich or poor." (*eleos*)

29. **1 Samuel 15:6.** He warned the Kenites, "Since you showed **kindness** to all the Israelites when they came out of Egypt, go on and leave! Get away from the Amalekites, or I'll sweep you away with them." So the Kenites withdrew from the Amalekites. (*eleos*)

30. **1 Samuel 20:8.** Deal **kindly** with your servant, for you have brought me into a covenant with you before the LORD. If I have done anything wrong, then kill me yourself; why take me to your father? (*eleos*)

31. **1 Samuel 20:14.** If I continue to live, show me **kindness** from the LORD, but if I die, . . . (*eleos*)

32. **1 Samuel 20:15.** . . . don't ever withdraw your **kindness** from my household—not even when the LORD cuts off every one of David's enemies from the face of the earth. (*eleos*)

33. **2 Samuel 2:5.** David sent messengers to the men of Jabesh-gilead and said to them, "The LORD bless you, because you have shown this **kindness** to Saul your lord when you buried him." (*eleos*)

34. **2 Samuel 2:6.** Now, may the LORD show **kindness** and faithfulness to you, and I will also show the same goodness to you because you have done this deed. (*eleos*)

35. **2 Samuel 3:8.** All this time I've been **loyal** to the family of your father Saul, to his brothers, and to his friends and haven't betrayed you to David, but now you accuse me of wrongdoing with this woman! (*eleos*)

36. **2 Samuel 7:15.** But my **faithful love** will never leave him as it did when I removed it from Saul, whom I removed from before you. (*eleos*)

37. **2 Samuel 9:1.** David asked, "Is there anyone remaining from the family of Saul I can show **kindness** to for Jonathan's sake?" (*eleos*)

38. **2 Samuel 9:3.** So the king asked, "Is there anyone left of Saul's family that I can show the **kindness** of God to?" (*eleos*)

39. **2 Samuel 9:7.** "Don't be afraid," David said to him, "since I intend to show you **kindness** for the sake of your father Jonathan." (*eleos*)

40. **2 Samuel 10:2.** Then David said, "I'll show **kindness** to Hanun son of Nahash, just as his father showed **kindness** to me." (*eleos*)

41. **2 Samuel 15:20.** Go back and take your brothers with you. May the LORD show you **kindness** and faithfulness. (*eleos*)

42. **2 Samuel 16:17.** "Is this your **loyalty** to your friend?" Absalom asked Hushai. "Why didn't you go with your friend?" (*eleos*)

43. **2 Samuel 22:26.** With the **faithful** / you prove yourself **faithful**, / with the blameless / you prove yourself blameless.

44. **2 Samuel 22:51.** He is a tower of salvation for his king; / he shows **loyalty** to his anointed, / to David and his descendants forever. (*eleos*)

45. **1 Kings 2:7.** Show **kindness** to the sons of Barzillai the Gileadite and let them be among those who eat at your table because they supported me when I fled from your brother Absalom. (*eleos*)

46. **1 Kings 3:6.** You have shown great and **faithful love** to your servant, my father David, because he walked before you in faithfulness, righteousness, and integrity. You have continued this great and **faithful love** for him by giving him a son to sit on his throne, as it is today.

47. **1 Kings 4:10.** Ben-**hesed**, in Arubboth (he had Socoh and the whole land of Hepher).

48. **1 Kings 8:23.** LORD God of Israel, / there is no God like you / in heaven above or on earth below, / who keeps the **gracious covenant** / with your servants who walk before you / with all their heart.

49. **1 Kings 20:31.** His servants said to him, "Consider this: we have heard that the kings of the house of Israel are **merciful** kings. So let's put sackcloth around our waists and ropes around our heads, and let's go out to the king of Israel. Perhaps he will spare your life."

50. **1 Chronicles 3:20.** And five others—Hashubah, Ohel, Berechiah, Hasadiah, and Jushab-**hesed**.

51. **1 Chronicles 16:34.** Give thanks to the Lord, for he is good; / his **faithful love** endures forever. (*eleos*)

52. **1 Chronicles 16:41.** With them were Heman, Jeduthun, and the rest who were chosen and designated by name to give thanks to the Lord—for his **faithful love** endures forever. (*eleos*)

53. **1 Chronicles 17:13.** I will be his father, and he will be my son. I will not remove my **faithful love** from him as I removed it from the one who was before you. (*eleos*)

54. **1 Chronicles 19:2.** Then David said, "I'll show **kindness** to Hanun son of Nahash, because his father showed **kindness** to me." (*eleos*)

55. **2 Chronicles 1:8.** And Solomon said to God: "You have shown great and **faithful love** to my father David, and you have made me king in his place." (*eleos*)

56. **2 Chronicles 5:13.** They raised their voices, accompanied by trumpets, cymbals, and musical instruments, in praise to the Lord: For he is good; / his **faithful love** endures forever.

57. **2 Chronicles 6:14.** Lord God of Israel, / there is no God like you / in heaven or on earth, / who keeps his **gracious covenant** / with your servants who walk before you / with all their heart. (*eleos*)

58. **2 Chronicles 6:42.** Lord God, do not reject your anointed one; / remember the **promises** to your servant David. (*eleos*)

59. **2 Chronicles 7:3.** All the Israelites were watching when the fire descended and the glory of the Lord came on the temple. They bowed down on the pavement with their faces to the ground. They worshiped and praised the Lord: For he is good, / for his **faithful love** endures forever. (*eleos*)

60. **2 Chronicles 7:6.** The Levites had the musical instruments of the LORD, which King David had made to give thanks to the LORD—"for his **faithful love** endures forever"—when he offered praise with them. (*eleos*)

61. **2 Chronicles 20:21.** When they went out in front of the armed forces, they kept singing: Give thanks to the LORD, / for his **faithful love** endures forever.

62. **2 Chronicles 24:22.** King Joash didn't remember the **kindness** that Zechariah's father Jehoiada had extended to him, but killed his son. (*eleos*)

63. **2 Chronicles 32:32.** As for the rest of the events of Hezekiah's reign and his deeds of **faithful love**, note that they are written in the Visions of the Prophet Isaiah son of Amoz, and in the Book of the Kings of Judah and Israel.

64. **2 Chronicles 35:26.** The rest of the events of Josiah's reign, along with his deeds of **faithful love** according to what is written in the law of the LORD. (*elpis*)

65. **Ezra 3:11.** They sang with praise and thanksgiving to the LORD: "For he is good; his **faithful love** to Israel endures forever." Then all the people gave a great shout of praise to the LORD because the foundation of the LORD's house had been laid. (*eleos*)

66. **Ezra 7:28.** And who has shown **favor** to me before the king, his counselors, and all his powerful officers. (*eleos*)

67. **Ezra 9:9.** Though we are slaves, our God has not abandoned us in our slavery. He has extended **grace** to us in the presence of the Persian kings, giving us relief, so that we can rebuild the house of our God and repair its ruins, to give us a wall in Judah and Jerusalem. (*eleos*)

68. **Nehemiah 1:5.** LORD, the God of the heavens, the great and awe-inspiring God who keeps his **gracious covenant** with those who love him and keep his commands.

69. **Nehemiah 9:17.** They became stiff-necked and appointed a leader / to return to their slavery in Egypt. / But you are a forgiving God, / gracious and compassionate, / slow to anger and abounding in **faithful love**, / and you did not abandon them.

70. **Nehemiah 9:32.** So now, our God—the great, mighty, / and awe-inspiring God who keeps his **gracious covenant**— / do not view lightly all the hardships that have afflicted us, / our kings and leaders, / our priests and prophets, / our ancestors and all your people, / from the days of the Assyrian kings until today.

71. **Nehemiah 13:14.** Remember me for this, my God, and don't erase the deeds of **faithful love** I have done for the house of my God and for its services.

72. **Nehemiah 13:22.** Remember me for this also, my God, and look on me with compassion according to the abundance of your **faithful love.**

73. **Esther 2:9.** The young woman pleased him and gained his **favor** so that he accelerated the process of the beauty treatments and the special diet that she received. (*charis*)

74. **Esther 2:17.** The king loved Esther more than all the other women. She won more **favor** and approval from him than did any of the other virgins. (*charis*)

75. **Job 6:14.** A despairing man should receive **loyalty** from his friends, / even if he abandons the fear of the Almighty. (*eleos*)

76. **Job 10:12.** You gave me life and **faithful love**, / and your care has guarded my life. (*eleos*)

77. **Job 37:13.** He causes this to happen for punishment, / for his land, or for his **faithful love**. (*eleos*)

78. **Psalm 5:7.** But I enter your house / by the abundance of your **faithful love**; / I bow down toward your holy temple / in reverential awe of you. (*eleos*)

79. **Psalm 6:4.** Turn, LORD! Rescue me; / save me because of your **faithful love**. (*eleos*)

80. **Psalm 13:6.** I will sing to the LORD / because he has treated me **generously**. (*eleos*)

81. **Psalm 17:7.** Display the wonders of your **faithful love**. (*eleos*)

82. **Psalm 18:25.** With the **faithful** / you prove yourself **faithful**, / with the blameless / you prove yourself blameless. (*eleos*)

83. **Psalm 18:50.** He gives great victories to his king; / he shows **loyalty** to his anointed, / to David and his descendants forever. (*eleos*)

84. **Psalm 21:7.** For the king relies on the LORD; / through the **faithful love** of the Most High / he is not shaken. (*eleos*)

85. **Psalm 23:6.** Only goodness and **faithful love** will pursue me / all the days of my life, / and I will dwell in the house of the LORD / as long as I live. (*eleos*)

86. **Psalm 25:6.** Remember, LORD, your compassion / and your **faithful love**, / for they have existed from antiquity. (*eleos*)

87. **Psalm 25:7.** Do not remember the sins of my youth / or my acts of rebellion; / in keeping with your **faithful love**, remember me / because of your goodness, LORD. (*eleos*)

88. **Psalm 25:10.** All the LORD's ways show **faithful love** and truth / to those who keep his covenant and decrees. (*eleos*)

89. **Psalm 26:3.** For your **faithful love** guides me, / and I live by your truth. (*eleos*)

90. **Psalm 31:7.** I will rejoice and be glad in your **faithful love** / because you have seen my affliction. / You know the troubles of my soul. (*eleos*)

91. **Psalm 31:16.** Make your face shine on your servant; / save me by your **faithful love.** (*eleos*)

92. **Psalm 31:21** Blessed be the LORD, / for he has wondrously shown his **faithful love** to me / in a city under siege. (*eleos*)

93. **Psalm 32:10.** Many pains come to the wicked, / but the one who trusts in the LORD / will have **faithful love** surrounding him. (*eleos*)

94. **Psalm 33:5.** He loves righteousness and justice; / the earth is full of the LORD's **unfailing love.** (*eleos*)

95. **Psalm 33:18.** But look, the LORD keeps his eye on those who fear him— / those who depend on his **faithful love.** (*eleos*)

96. **Psalm 33:22.** May your **faithful love** rest on us, LORD, / for we put our hope in you. (*eleos*)

97. **Psalm 36:5.** LORD, your **faithful love** reaches to heaven, / your faithfulness to the clouds. (*eleos*)

98. **Psalm 36:7.** How priceless your **faithful love** is, God! / People take refuge in the shadow of your wings. (*eleos*)

99. **Psalm 36:10.** Spread your **faithful love** over those who know you, / and your righteousness over the upright in heart. (*eleos*)

100. **Psalm 40:10.** I did not hide your righteousness in my heart; / I spoke about your faithfulness and salvation; / I did not conceal your **constant love** and truth / from the great assembly. (*eleos*)

101. **Psalm 40:11.** LORD, you do not withhold your compassion from me. / Your **constant love** and truth will always guard me. (*eleos*)

102. **Psalm 42:8.** The LORD will send his **faithful love** by day; / his song will be with me in the night— / a prayer to the God of my life. (*eleos*)

103. **Psalm 44:26.** Rise up! Help us! / Redeem us because of your **faithful love.** (*onomatos*)

104. **Psalm 48:9.** God, within your temple, / we contemplate your **faithful love.** (*eleos*)

105. **Psalm 51:1.** Be gracious to me, God, / according to your **faithful love**; / according to your abundant compassion, / blot out my rebellion. (*eleos*)

106. **Psalm 52:1.** Why boast about evil, you hero! / God's **faithful love** is constant. (The LXX does not translate.)

107. **Psalm 52:8.** But I am like a flourishing olive tree / in the house of God; / I trust in God's **faithful love** forever and ever. (*eleos*)

108. **Psalm 57:3.** God sends his **faithful love** and truth. (*eleos*)

109. **Psalm 57:10.** For your **faithful love** is as high as the heavens; / your faithfulness reaches the clouds. (*eleos*)

110. **Psalm 59:10.** My **faithful** God will come to meet me; / God will let me look down on my adversaries. (*eleos*)

111. **Psalm 59:16.** But I will sing of your strength / and will joyfully proclaim / your **faithful love** in the morning. (*eleos*)

112. **Psalm 59:17.** To you, my strength, I sing praises, / because God is my stronghold— / my **faithful** God. (*eleos*)

113. **Psalm 61:7.** May he sit enthroned before God forever. / Appoint **faithful love** and truth to guard him. (*eleos*)

114. **Psalm 62:12.** And **faithful love** belongs to you, LORD. / For you repay each according to his works. (*eleos*)

115. **Psalm 63:3.** My lips will glorify you / because your **faithful love** is better than life. (*eleos*)

116. **Psalm 66:20.** Blessed be God! / He has not turned away my prayer / or turned his **faithful love** from me. (*eleos*)

117. **Psalm 69:13.** But as for me, LORD, / my prayer to you is for a time of favor. / In your abundant, **faithful love**, God, / answer me with your sure salvation. (*eleos*)

118. **Psalm 69:16.** Answer me, LORD, / for your **faithful love** is good. / In keeping with your abundant compassion, / turn to me. (*eleos*)

119. **Psalm 77:8.** Has his **faithful love** ceased forever? / Is his promise at an end for all generations? (*eleos*)

120. **Psalm 85:7.** Show us your **faithful love,** LORD, / and give us your salvation. (*eleos*)

121. **Psalm 85:10. Faithful love** and truth will join together; / righteousness and peace will embrace. (*eleos*)

122. **Psalm 86:5.** For you, Lord, are kind and ready to forgive, / abounding in **faithful love** to all who call on you. (*eleos*)

123. **Psalm 86:13.** For your **faithful love** for me is great, / and you rescue my life from the depths of Sheol. (*eleos*)

124. **Psalm 86:15.** But you, Lord, are a compassionate and gracious God, / slow to anger and abounding in **faithful love** and truth. (*eleos*)

125. **Psalm 88:11.** Will your **faithful love** be declared in the grave, / your faithfulness in Abaddon? (*eleos*)

126. **Psalm 89:1.** I will sing about the LORD's **faithful love** forever; / I will proclaim your faithfulness to all generations / with my mouth. (*eleos*)

127. **Psalm 89:2.** For I will declare, / "**Faithful love** is built up forever; / you establish your faithfulness in the heavens." (*eleos*)

128. **Psalm 89:14.** Righteousness and justice are the foundation of your throne; / **faithful love** and truth go before you. (*eleos*)

129. **Psalm 89:24.** My faithfulness and **love** will be with him, / and through my name / his horn will be exalted. (*eleos*)

130. **Psalm 89:28.** I will always preserve my **faithful love** for him, / and my covenant with him will endure. (*eleos*)

131. **Psalm 89:33.** But I will not withdraw / my **faithful love** from him / or betray my faithfulness. (*eleos*)

132. **Psalm 89:49.** Lord, where are the former acts of your **faithful love** / that you swore to David in your faithfulness? (*eleos*)

133. **Psalm 90:14.** Satisfy us in the morning with your **faithful love** / so that we may shout with joy and be glad all our days. (*eleos*)

134. **Psalm 92:2.** To declare your **faithful love** in the morning / and your faithfulness at night. (*eleos*)

135. **Psalm 94:18.** If I say, "My foot is slipping," / your **faithful love** will support me, LORD. (*eleos*)

136. **Psalm 98:3.** He has remembered his **love** / and faithfulness to the house of Israel; / all the ends of the earth / have seen our God's victory. (*eleos*)

137. **Psalm 100:5.** For the LORD is good, and his **faithful love** endures forever; / his faithfulness, through all generations. (*eleos*)

138. **Psalm 101:1.** I will sing of **faithful love** and justice; / I will sing praise to you, LORD. (*eleos*)

139. **Psalm 103:4.** He redeems your life from the Pit; / he crowns you with **faithful love** and compassion. (*eleos*)

140. **Psalm 103:8.** The LORD is compassionate and gracious, / slow to anger and abounding in **faithful love.** (*eleos*)

141. **Psalm 103:11.** For as high as the heavens are above the earth, / so great is his **faithful love** / toward those who fear him. (*eleos*)

142. **Psalm 103:17.** But from eternity to eternity / the LORD's **faithful love** is toward those who fear him. (*eleos*)

143. **Psalm 106:1.** Hallelujah! / Give thanks to the LORD, for he is good; / his **faithful love** endures forever. (*eleos*)

144. **Psalm 106:7.** Our fathers in Egypt did not grasp / the significance of your wondrous works / or remember your many acts of **faithful love**; / instead, they rebelled by the sea—the Red Sea. (*eleos*)

145. **Psalm 106:45.** Remembered his covenant with them, / and relented according to the abundance / of his **faithful love.** (*eleos*)

146. **Psalm 107:1.** Give thanks to the LORD, for he is good; / his **faithful love** endures forever. (*eleos*)

147. **Psalm 107:8.** Let them give thanks to the LORD / for his **faithful love** / and his wondrous works for all humanity. (*eleos*)

148. **Psalm 107:15.** Let them give thanks to the LORD / for his **faithful love /** and his wondrous works for all humanity. (*eleos*)

149. **Psalm 107:21.** Let them give thanks to the LORD / for his **faithful love /** and his wondrous works for all humanity. (*eleos*)

150. **Psalm 107:31.** Let them give thanks to the LORD / for his **faithful love /** and his wondrous works for all humanity. (*eleos*)

151. **Psalm 107:43.** Let whoever is wise pay attention to these things / and consider the LORD's acts of **faithful love**. (*eleos*)

152. **Psalm 108:4.** For your **faithful love** is higher than the heavens, / and your faithfulness reaches to the clouds. (*eleos*)

153. **Psalm 109:12.** Let no one show him **kindness**, / and let no one be gracious to his fatherless children. (*eleos*)

154. **Psalm 109:16.** For he did not think to show **kindness**, / but pursued the suffering, needy, and brokenhearted / in order to put them to death. (*eleos*)

155. **Psalm 109:21.** But you, LORD, my Lord, / deal kindly with me for your name's sake; / because your **faithful love** is good, rescue me. (*eleos*)

156. **Psalm 109:26.** Help me, LORD my God; / save me according to your **faithful love.** (*eleos*)

157. **Psalm 115:1.** Not to us, LORD, not to us, / but to your name give glory / because of your **faithful love**, because of your truth. (*eleos*)

158. **Psalm 117:2.** For his **faithful love** to us is great; / the LORD's faithfulness endures forever. / Hallelujah! (*eleos*)

159. **Psalm 118:1.** Give thanks to the LORD, for he is good; / his **faithful love** endures forever. (*eleos*)

160. **Psalm 118:2.** Let Israel say, / "His **faithful love** endures forever." (*eleos*)

161. **Psalm 118:3.** Let the house of Aaron say, / "His **faithful love** endures forever." (*eleos*)

162. **Psalm 118:4.** Let those who fear the LORD say, / "His **faithful love** endures forever." (*eleos*)

163. **Psalm 118:29** Give thanks to the LORD, for he is good; / his **faithful love** endures forever. (*eleos*)

164. **Psalm 119:41.** Let your **faithful love** come to me, LORD, / your salvation, as you promised. (*eleos*)

165. **Psalm 119:64.** LORD, the earth is filled with your **faithful love**; / teach me your statutes. (*eleos*)

166. **Psalm 119:76.** May your **faithful love** comfort me / as you promised your servant. (*eleos*)

167. **Psalm 119:88.** Give me life in accordance with your **faithful love**, / and I will obey the decree you have spoken. (*eleos*)

168. **Psalm 119:124.** Deal with your servant based on your **faithful love**; / teach me your statutes. (*eleos*)

169. **Psalm 119:149.** In keeping with your **faithful love**, hear my voice. / LORD, give me life in keeping with your justice. (*eleos*)

170. **Psalm 119:159.** Consider how I love your precepts; / LORD, give me life according to your **faithful love**. (*eleos*)

171. **Psalm 130:7.** Israel, put your hope in the LORD. / For there is **faithful love** with the LORD, / and with him is redemption in abundance. (*eleos*)

172. **Psalm 136:1.** Give thanks to the LORD, for he is good. / *His **faithful love** endures forever.* (*eleos*)

173. **Psalm 136:2.** Give thanks to the God of gods. / *His **faithful love** endures forever.* (*eleos*)

174. **Psalm 136:3.** Give thanks to the Lord of lords. / *His **faithful love** endures forever.* (*eleos*)

175. **Psalm 136:4.** He alone does great wonders. / *His **faithful love** endures forever.* (*eleos*)

176. **Psalm 136:5.** He made the heavens skillfully. / *His **faithful love** endures forever.* (*eleos*)

177. **Psalm 136:6.** He spread the land on the waters. / *His **faithful love** endures forever.* (*eleos*)

178. **Psalm 136:7.** He made the great lights: / *His **faithful love** endures forever.* (*eleos*)

179. **Psalm 136:8.** the sun to rule by day, / *His **faithful love** endures forever.* (*eleos*)

180. **Psalm 136:9.** the moon and stars to rule by night. / *His **faithful love** endures forever.* (*eleos*)

181. **Psalm 136:10.** He struck the firstborn of the Egyptians / *His **faithful love** endures forever.* (*eleos*)

182. **Psalm 136:11.** and brought Israel out from among them / *His **faithful love** endures forever.* (*eleos*)

183. **Psalm 136:12.** with a strong hand and outstretched arm. / *His **faithful love** endures forever.* (*eleos*)

184. **Psalm 136:13.** He divided the Red Sea / *His **faithful love** endures forever.* (*eleos*)

185. **Psalm 136:14.** and led Israel through, / *His **faithful love** endures forever.* (*eleos*)

186. **Psalm 136:15.** but hurled Pharaoh and his army into the Red Sea. / *His **faithful love** endures forever.* (*eleos*)

187. **Psalm 136:16.** He led his people in the wilderness. / *His **faithful love** endures forever.* (*eleos*)

188. **Psalm 136:17.** He struck down great kings / *His **faithful love** endures forever.* (*eleos*)

189. **Psalm 136:18.** and slaughtered famous kings— / *His **faithful** love endures forever.* (*eleos*)

190. **Psalm 136:19.** Sihon king of the Amorites / *His **faithful love** endures forever.* (*eleos*)

191. **Psalm 136:20.** and Og king of Bashan— / *His **faithful love** endures forever.* (*eleos*)

192. **Psalm 136:21.** and gave their land as an inheritance, / *His **faithful love** endures forever.* (*eleos*)

193. **Psalm 136:22.** an inheritance to Israel his servant. / *His **faithful love** endures forever.* (*eleos*)

194. **Psalm 136:23.** He remembered us in our humiliation / *His **faithful love** endures forever.* (*eleos*)

195. **Psalm 136:24.** and rescued us from our foes. / *His **faithful love** endures forever.* (*eleos*)

196. **Psalm 136:25.** He gives food to every creature. / *His **faithful love** endures forever.* (*eleos*)

197. **Psalm 136:26.** Give thanks to the God of heaven! / *His **faithful love** endures forever.* (*eleos*)

198. **Psalm 138:2.** I will bow down toward your holy temple / and give thanks to your name / for your **constant love** and truth. (*eleos*)

199. **Psalm 138:8.** The LORD will fulfill his purpose for me. / LORD, your **faithful love** endures forever; / do not abandon the work of your hands. (*eleos*)

200. **Psalm 141:5.** Let the righteous one strike me— / it is an act of **faithful love;** / let him rebuke me— / it is oil for my head; / let me not refuse it. (*eleos*)

201. **Psalm 143:8.** Let me experience / your **faithful love** in the morning, / for I trust in you. (*eleos*)

202. **Psalm 143:12.** And in your **faithful love** destroy my enemies. / Wipe out all those who attack me, / for I am your servant. (*eleos*)

203. **Psalm 144:2.** He is my **faithful love** and my fortress, / my stronghold and my deliverer. (*eleos*)

204. **Psalm 145:8.** The LORD is gracious and compassionate, / slow to anger and great in **faithful love**. (*eleos*)

205. **Psalm 147:11.** The LORD values those who fear him, / those who put their hope in his **faithful love.** (*eleos*)

206. **Proverbs 3:3.** Never let **loyalty** and faithfulness leave you. / Tie them around your neck; / write them on the tablet of your heart. (*eleos*)

207. **Proverbs 11:17.** A **kind** man benefits himself, / but a cruel person brings ruin on himself. (*eleos*)

208. **Proverbs 14:22.** Don't those who plan evil go astray? / But those who plan good find **loyalty** and faithfulness. (*eleos*)

209. **Proverbs 14:34.** Righteousness exalts a nation, / but sin is a **disgrace** to any people.

210. **Proverbs 16:6.** Iniquity is atoned for by **loyalty** and faithfulness, / and one turns from evil by the fear of the LORD. (*eleos*)

211. **Proverbs 19:22.** What is desirable in a person is his **fidelity**; / better to be a poor person than a liar. (*dikaios*)

212. **Proverbs 20:6.** Many a person proclaims his own **loyalty**, / but who can find a trustworthy person? (*eleos*)

213. **Proverbs 20:28. Loyalty** and faithfulness guard a king; / through **loyalty** he maintains his throne. (*eleos*)

214. **Proverbs 21:21.** The one who pursues righteousness and **faithful love** / will find life, righteousness, and honor. (*eleos*)

215. **Proverbs 25:10.** Otherwise, the one who hears will **disgrace** you, / and you'll never live it down. (The LXX omits this verse.)

216. **Proverbs 31:26.** Her mouth speaks wisdom, / and **loving instruction** is on her tongue. (The LXX omits this verse.)

217. **Isaiah 16:5.** A throne will be established in **love**, / and one will sit on it faithfully / in the tent of David, / judging and pursuing what is right, / quick to execute justice. (*eleos*)

218. **Isaiah 40:6.** A voice was saying, "Cry out!" / Another said, "What should I cry out?" / "All humanity is grass, / and all its **goodness** is like the flower of the field." (*doxa*)

219. **Isaiah 54:8.** "In a surge of anger / I hid my face from you for a moment, / but I will have compassion on you / with **everlasting love**," / says the LORD your Redeemer. (*eleos*)

220. **Isaiah 54:10.** "Though the mountains move / and the hills shake, / my **love** will not be removed from you / and my covenant of peace will not be shaken," / says your compassionate LORD. (*eleos*)

221. **Isaiah 55:3.** Pay attention and come to me; / listen, so that you will live. / I will make a permanent covenant with you / on the basis of the **faithful kindnesses** of David. (*hosia*)

222. **Isaiah 57:1.** The righteous person perishes, / and no one takes it to heart; / the **faithful** are taken away, / with no one realizing / that the righteous person is taken away / because of evil. (*dikaios*)

223. **Isaiah 63:7.** I will make known the LORD's **faithful love** / and the LORD's praiseworthy acts, / because of all the LORD has done for us— / even the many good things / he has done for the

house of Israel, / which he did for them based on his compassion / and the abundance of his **faithful love**. (*eleos*)

224. **Jeremiah 2:2.** Go and announce directly to Jerusalem that this is what the LORD says: I remember the **loyalty** of your youth, / your love as a bride— / how you followed me in the wilderness, / in a land not sown. (*eleos*)

225. **Jeremiah 9:24.** But the one who boasts should boast in this: that he understands and knows me— / that I am the LORD, showing **faithful love**, / justice, and righteousness on the earth, / for I delight in these things. / This is the LORD's declaration. (*eleos*)

226. **Jeremiah 16:5.** For this is what the LORD says: Don't enter a house where a mourning feast is taking place. Don't go to lament or sympathize with them, for I have removed my peace from these people as well as my **faithful love** and compassion. (The LXX omits the last section of this verse.)

227. **Jeremiah 31:3.** The LORD appeared to him from far away. / I have loved you with an everlasting love; / therefore, I have continued to extend **faithful love** to you. (*eleos*)

228. **Jeremiah 32:18.** You show **faithful love** to thousands but lay the fathers' iniquity on their sons' laps after them, great and mighty God whose name is the LORD of Armies. (*eleos*)

229. **Jeremiah 33:11.** A sound of joy and gladness, the voice of the groom and the bride, and the voice of those saying, Give thanks to the LORD of Armies, / for the LORD is good; / his **faithful love** endures forever.

230. **Lamentations 3:22.** Because of the LORD's **faithful love** / we do not perish, / for his mercies never end. (The LXX omits this verse.)

231. **Lamentations 3:32.** Even if he causes suffering, / he will show compassion / according to the abundance of his **faithful love**. (*eleos*)

232. **Daniel 1:9.** God had granted Daniel **kindness** and compassion from the chief eunuch. (*eleos*)

233. **Daniel 9:4.** I prayed to the LORD my God and confessed: Ah, Lord—the great and awe-inspiring God who keeps his **gracious covenant** with those who love him and keep his commands. (*eleos*)

234. **Hosea 2:19.** I will take you to be my wife forever. / I will take you to be my wife in righteousness, / justice, **love**, and compassion. (*eleos*)

235. **Hosea 4:1.** Hear the word of the LORD, people of Israel, / for the LORD has a case / against the inhabitants of the land: / There is no truth, no **faithful love**, / and no knowledge of God in the land! (*eleos*)

236. **Hosea 6:4.** What am I going to do with you, Ephraim? / What am I going to do with you, Judah? / Your **love** is like the morning mist / and like the early dew that vanishes. (*eleos*)

237. **Hosea 6:6.** For I desire **faithful love** and not sacrifice, / the knowledge of God rather than burnt offerings. (*eleos*)

238. **Hosea 10:12.** Sow righteousness for yourselves / and reap **faithful love**; / break up your unplowed ground. (The LXX inserts a completely different phrase.)

239. **Hosea 12:6.** But you must return to your God. / Maintain **love** and justice, / and always put your hope in God. (*eleos*)

240. **Joel 2:13.** Tear your hearts, / not just your clothes, / and return to the LORD your God. / For he is gracious and compassionate,

/ slow to anger, abounding in **faithful love**, / and he relents from sending disaster. (*eleos*)

241. **Jonah 2:8.** Those who cherish worthless idols / abandon their **faithful love.** (*eleos*)

242. **Jonah 4:2.** He prayed to the LORD: "Please, LORD, isn't this what I thought while I was still in my own country? That's why I fled toward Tarshish in the first place. I knew that you are a gracious and compassionate God, slow to anger, abounding in **faithful love**, and one who relents from sending disaster." (*eleos*)

243. **Micah 6:8.** Mankind, he has told each of you what is good / and what it is the LORD requires of you: / to act justly, / to love **faithfulness**, / and to walk humbly with your God. (*eleos*)

244. **Micah 7:18.** Who is a God like you, / forgiving iniquity and passing over rebellion / for the remnant of his inheritance? / He does not hold on to his anger forever / because he delights in **faithful love.** (*eleos*)

245. **Micah 7:20.** You will show loyalty to Jacob / and **faithful love** to Abraham, / as you swore to our fathers / from days long ago. (*eleos*)

246. **Zechariah 7:9.** The LORD of Armies says this: "Make fair decisions. Show **faithful love** and compassion to one another." (*eleos*)

GREEK WORDS USED BY THE SEPTUAGINT

- mercy (*eleos*), 197
- righteousness (*dikaiosune*), 6
- grace (*charis*), 2

- hope (*elpis*), 1
- name(sake) (*onomatia*), 1
- glory (*doxa*), 1
- holy (*hosia*), 1

APPENDIX B

COMPARISON OF TRANSLATIONS

This list shows the English words several versions use to translate *hesed*, along with the number of times each occurs.

KING JAMES VERSION (KJV)

mercy/mercies, 149	favor, 2	good deeds, 1
kindness/kindly, 41	goodness, 2	wicked thing, 1
loving-kindness, 25	pity, 1	

NEW INTERNATIONAL VERSION (NIV)

love, 118	mercy, 4	merciful, 1
kindness, 41	unfailing kindness, 4	disgrace, 1
unfailing love, 37	favor, 3	treated well, 1
covenant of love, 5	devotion, 2	loyalty, 1

AMERICAN STANDARD VERSION (ASV)

loving-kindness, 175	good deeds, 4
kindness, 43	shameful thing, 1
mercy, 6	

ENGLISH STANDARD VERSION (ESV)

steadfast love, 193	love, 2	faithfulness, 1
kindness, 9	merciful, 1	favor, 1
kindly, 6	beauty, 1	disgrace, 1
loyalty, 5	righteous, 1	
favor, 2	devotion, 1	

HOLMAN CHRISTIAN STANDARD BIBLE (HCSB)

faithful love, 135	favor, 3	fidelity, 1
love, 31	covenant loyalty, 2	loving instruction, 1
kindness, 26	well, 1	goodness, 1
loyalty, 9	merciful, 1	righteousness, 1
gracious covenant, 4	grace, 1	disgrace, 1

NEW LIVING TRANSLATION (NLT)

unfailing love, 118	favor, 4	loyal, 3
kindness, 7	kind, 4	devotion, 2
love, 7	mercy, 3	good, 1
great love, 4	loyalty, 3	shameful disgrace, 1

THE MESSAGE

love, 114	graciously, 1	covenant friend, 1
loyal (in) love, 12	merciful love, 1	covenant friendship, 1
kindness, 6	unswervingly loyal, 1	honoring, 1
marvelous love, 4	disgrace, 1	sticking by, 1
generous, 3	mercy, 1	godly kindness, 1
favor, 2	loyal mercy, 1	something special, 1
well, 2	good, 1	grace, 1
stick with, 2	expression of love, 1	devotion, 1
immense favor, 1	stick with me, 1	play by the rules, 1

extravagantly generous, 1

loyal service, 1

never quit loving, 1

good graces, 1

tons of love, 1

devoted work, 1

special interest, 1

beloved, 1

affectionate satisfaction, 1

love-in-action, 1

generous in love, 1

dependable love, 1

largesse, 1

deep love, 1

wonderful love, 1

merciful love, 1

true love, 1

help, 1

weak, 1

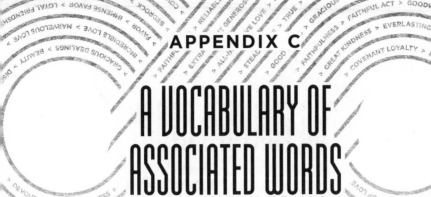

APPENDIX C

A VOCABULARY OF ASSOCIATED WORDS

These are the eight words associated with *hesed*:

- truth, *emet* (אמת) (Gen 24:27, 49; 32:10; 47:29; Ex 34:6; Josh 2:14; 2 Sam 2:6; 15:20; Ps 25:10; 40:10; 57:3; 61:7; 69:13; 85:10; 86:15; 89:14; Prov 3:3; 14:22; 16:6; 20:28; Hos 4:1)

- mercy/compassion, *raham* (רחם) (Ps 25:6; 103:4; Jer 16:5; Dan 1:9; Hos 2:19; Zech 7:9)

- covenant, *berith* (ברית) (Deut 7:9, 12; 1 Kings 8:23; 2 Chron 6:14; Neh 1:5; Dan 9:4)

- justice, *mishpat* (משפט) (Ps 100:5; Jer 9:24; Hos 12:6)

- faithfulness, *amuna* (אמונה) (Ps 89:24; 98:3)

- goodness, *tov* (טוב) (Ps 23:6; 86:5)

- favor, *hen* (חן) (Esther 2:17)

- righteousness, *tsadik* (צדק) (Prov 21:21)

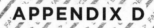

APPENDIX D

FOR FURTHER STUDY

HESED IN THE OLD TESTAMENT

1. Jacob's realization of his need for hesed: Genesis 32:10

2. God's unfailing love to his unworthy people: Exodus 15:13

3. Jonathan's plea to David: 1 Samuel 20:8, 14, 15

4. The hesed of burial: 2 Samuel 2:5

5. God's promise to David of a kingdom rooted in hesed: 2 Samuel 7:15; 1 Chronicles 17:13; Psalm 89:33

6. Job expects it from his friends: Job 6:14

7. An abundance of love over punishment: Exodus 20:5-6; Deuteronomy 5:9-10

8. Covenant works only because of God's hesed: Deuteronomy 7:9, 12; 2 Samuel 22:51; Nehemiah 9:16-17, 32

9. Hesed even to slaves: Ezra 9:9

10. Hesed gives us access to God's house: Psalm 5:7; Psalm 23:6; Psalm 48:9

11. Hesed as a basis for hope: Psalm 33:18, 22; Psalm 147:11

12. Hesed is better than life: Psalm 63:3

13. Hesed as a basis for the covenant: Psalm 89:28; Psalm 106:45

14. Hesed as a basis for comfort: Psalm 119:76

15. Hesed as our most basic desire: Proverbs 19:22

16. Hesed represents the turning point of lament: Psalm 13:5; Lamentations 3:22

17. Hesed as a foundation for our union with God: Hosea 2:19

18. Hesed defines what God wants from his people: Hosea 6:6; Micah 6:8 (compare Psalm 51)

19. Jonah as a hater of hesed: Jonah 4:2 (compare the elder brother in the parable of the prodigal son, Luke 15:11-32)

HESED IN THE LIFE OF JESUS

1. Parables of hesed: the eccentric employer, Matthew 20:15; the two debtors, Luke 7:47; the good Samaritan, Luke 10:36-37; the prodigal son, Luke 15:20

2. The perfect prayer of Bartimaeus: Mark 10:47 (compare the ten lepers of Luke 17:13)

3. The theme of Mary's song: Luke 1:50, 54-55

4. Peter, hesed, and the new birth: 1 Peter 1:3

5. James and the triumph of mercy: James 2:13

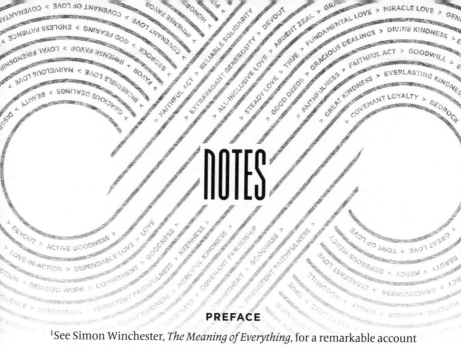

NOTES

PREFACE

[1]See Simon Winchester, *The Meaning of Everything*, for a remarkable account of the origin of the *Oxford English Dictionary* (Oxford: Oxford University Press, 2003).

INTRODUCTION

[1]Most Hebrew words are pronounced with the stress on the final syllable, but with words that have two segols (the vowel pointings beneath the consonants) in a row you place the emphasis on the first syllable.

[2]*Hesed* is often translated "disgrace" in these three passages: "If a man marries his sister, whether his father's daughter or his mother's daughter, and they have sexual relations, it is *hesed*" (Lev 20:17). "Righteousness exalts a nation, / but sin is *hesed* to any people" (Prov 14:34). "Make your case with your opponent without revealing another's secret; otherwise, the one who hears will *hesed* you, and you'll never live it down" (Prov 25:9-10).

That one of the defining characteristics of God, appearing over two hundred times in the Hebrew Bible, could in three instances be translated "disgrace" or "shame" should bother us. If we are to be serious students of the word *hesed*, we need to try to understand this phenomenon. There are basically four explanations:

1. It's the wrong word. The great rabbi Mosche ben Girondi, known simply as the Ramban, claims that the word in the original text was not *hesed* but in fact the Aramaic word *chisudo*, which means "shame." Given his stature as the most famous medieval Jewish scholar, this argument is widely accepted.

2. It's the right word, but mistranslated. In this view (also found in the rabbi's) *hesed* does not refer to incest but to "the inherent bond of kindness between brother and sister." This argument becomes terribly convoluted and almost impossible to follow.

3. Hesed has been misapplied. Samson Raphael Hirsch, a famous German rabbi from the nineteenth century, in his commentary on Vayikra 20:17 says, "If one chooses to act with hesed one is accepting to go beyond the call of duty. [But] if one forces another to act with hesed, forcing the other to do beyond the call of duty, one is grossly imposing upon the other for the overextended benefit of self" (Rav Samson Raphael Hirsch, *The Hirsch Chumash: Vayikra*, 2 vols. [Nanuet, NY: Feldheim and Judaica Press, 2008]). In other words, if you try to force someone to do hesed, it becomes negative.

4. It is a simple phenomenon of language. Again, language is fluid; words are always shifting in pronunciation and meaning. One interesting and not infrequent facet of language is that words can develop two contrary meanings. In English, for example, *cleave* can mean "to separate" or "to join"; *clip* can mean "to cut apart" or "to fasten"; *fast* may be "rapid" or "unmoving"; and *oversight* can refer to "care" or "error." There is at least one example of this phenomenon in Hebrew: *berech*, which means "to bless," is used in Job 2:9 to mean "to curse."

1 OPENING THE DOOR

[1]See William Plummer, "In a Supreme Act of Forgiveness, a Kentucky Couple 'Adopts' the Man Who Killed Their Son," *People*, August 26, 1985, http://people.com/archive/in-a-supreme-act-of-forgiveness-a-kentucky-couple-adopts-the-man-who-killed-their-son-vol-24-no-9.

[2]One of the best accounts of Keshia Thomas's story is Catherine Wynne, "The Teenager Who Saved a Man with an SS Tattoo," BBC News, October 29, 2013, www.bbc.com/news/magazine-24653643.

2 THE DEFINITIVE ENCOUNTER

[1]The Thirteen Attributes of Mercy are (1) the LORD (*JHWH*), (2) the LORD (*JHWH*), (3) God (*El*), (4) compassionate (*rahum*), (5) gracious (*vhanun*), (6) slow to anger (*apayim*), (7) abundant in kindness (*vrav hesed*), (8) truth (*vemet*), (9) preserver of kindness (*notzeir hesed la alafin*), (10) forgiver of iniquity (*nosei avron*), (11) forgiver of willful sin (*pasha*), (12) forgiver of error (*v hata 'ah*), (13) who clears or cleanses (*vnakah*).

[2]Jonathan Sacks, *To Heal a Fractured World: The Ethics of Responsibility* (New York: Schocken Books, 2005), 149.

3 SLOW TO ANGER

[1]Katharine Doob Sakenfeld, "Problem of Divine Forgiveness in Numbers 14," *Catholic Biblical Quarterly* 37, no. 3 (1975): 325.

[2]C. S. Lewis, *The Great Divorce* (New York: HarperCollins, 2015), 72.

4 LIKE NO OTHER GOD

[1]Sakenfeld points out that the Semitic root of *hesed*, when it appears in other languages, always takes on a very different meaning. Katharine Doob Sakenfeld, "Problem of Divine Forgiveness in Numbers 14," *Catholic Biblical Quarterly* 37, no. 3 (1975): 19.

[2]In some of the ancient sources there are songs that praise the god for hearing prayers and being "rich in love." In a poem to Baal, one character is described as "kindly" (James Pritchard, *Anthology of the Texts from the Ancient Near East* [Princeton, NJ: Princeton University Press, 2011], 129). One Akkadian hymn to Ishtar describes her as "paying heed to compassion" (Pritchard, *Anthology*, 341). And one obscure Etruscan deity, Voltumna, is sometimes listed as the goddess of kindness, but virtually nothing is known about her. In Pritchard's 474-page *Anthology*, the word *kind* or *kindness* does not appear.

6 A PRAYER OF HONEST RAGE

[1]It is impossible to specifically identify the person the psalm is directed against. Some have suggested it might have been Saul. Compare Psalm 55, where David is also lamenting a close friendship that was betrayed.

[2]Walter Brueggemann, "Psalm 109: Three Times 'Steadfast Love,'" *Word and World* 5, no. 2 (1985).

7 WHEN DINAH HELD MY HAND

[1]I made a brief reference to this moment in my book *A Better Freedom* (Downers Grove, IL: InterVarsity Press, 2009), 17-19.

[2]Michael Card, "When Dinah Held My Hand," copyright 2018 Covenant Artists.

8 THE HESEDS OF DAVID

[1]*Hesed* occurs only eighteen times in plural form: Gen 32:10; 2 Chron 6:42; 32:32; 35:26; Neh 13:14; Ps 17:7; 25:6; 89:2, 50; 106:7, 45; 107:43; 119:41; Is 55:3;

63:7 (2x); Lam 3:22, 32. The plural indicates "a lot of." *Racham*, "tender
mercy," is frequently rendered in the plural as *rachamim* or "tender
mercies." David uses this plural form only twice in his writings (Ps 17; 25).
[2]The idea of reciprocity implies a level of expectation. If you are the recipient
of hesed, it is expected that you will reciprocate. This represents a point of
tension with our working definition, "When the person from whom I have
a right to expect nothing gives me everything." This goes to show that there
is no single adequate definition of this indefinable word.
[3]A charming story from the Talmud concerning the great Aqiba's (normally
spelled Akiva) daughter and the snake reveals how early Judaism (Akiva
was born about twenty years after Jesus' resurrection) thought about the
principle of spiritual reciprocity, more specifically the unique reciprocity
connected to hesed.

> Rabbi Aqiba had a daughter, and the soothsayers predicted that on
> the day on which she should enter the garden a snake would bite her
> and she would die. He was very much troubled on that account.
>
> One day his daughter took off her headdress in the garden, and the
> needle protruding from it stuck on the side of the fence where a snake
> happened to be, piercing the eye of the snake, the latter was killed.
>
> When R. Aqiba's daughter went back to the house the snake
> dragged after her. Asked R. Aqiba, "What didst thou do today to
> escape death?"
>
> And she answered: "At dawn a man came to the door begging
> bread. Everybody, however, was at the table, and no one heard him but
> myself. I took my own meal, that thou gavest me and gave it to him."
>
> Said R. Aqiba: "Thou didst an act of charity, and this saved thee
> from death." He then went forth and preached, that charity may be
> the cause of saving a man's life. (Talmud Shabbat 156b)

10 MOSES: "IN THE MORNING"

[1]The same sort of thing happens with the familiar word *shalom*. In modern
Hebrew it functionally means "hello." In fact, modern dictionaries and
language courses will teach you that is the meaning. But everyone knows
the literal meaning is "peace." I like to believe that even to those who
only mean "hello," a little bit of peace is passed along via the word
shalom. (This is similar to the English *goodbye*, which originally meant
"God be with you.")

²There is a tradition recorded in Genesis Rabba 22 that the psalm was originally written by Adam, who was repenting for blaming Eve, and that Moses
simply found it.

11 JEREMIAH: "I AM HESED"

¹Compare Psalm 145:17: "The LORD is righteous in all his ways / and faithful
in all his acts."

12 HOSEA: A NOVEL OF HESED

¹Hosea's marriage to Gomer is referred to as "prophetic activity" in academic
circles. Many of the prophets demonstrate this sort of parabolic behavior.
Ezekiel symbolically eats a scroll in Ezekiel 3:1-3 and cuts his hair in 5:1-17,
all trying to make a point for God in a way that would capture people's attention. Jeremiah prophetically breaks a flask and wears a linen loincloth
(Jer 13:1-11; 19:1-13). But no one else was called to act out a prophetic message
to the extent that Hosea was. The message was so vital that Hosea was
called to communicate it in the most dramatic way: God loves his people
with an intensity that can be reflected only in the image of marriage.
Other examples of prophetic activity include Ezekiel 4:1-3, an iron pan as
a wall of iron signifying the coming siege of Jerusalem; Ezekiel 12:1-16, the
prophet packs and moves out in the people's sight; Ezekiel 12:17-20, the
prophet eats and drinks with anxious shaking; Ezekiel 24:1-7, a boiling pot;
Ezekiel 37:15-23, two sticks for the uniting of Judah and Israel; and 1 Kings
11:30-40; 2 Kings 13:15-19; Isaiah 20:1-6; Jeremiah 25:15-29; Jeremiah 27:1–
28:17; Jeremiah 43:8-13; Jeremiah 51:62-64; Mark 11:15-17; John 8:2-11; Acts
21:10-11.

²Michael Card, "Gomer's Song," copyright 1992 Sparrow Records.

13 HESED AND TRUTH

¹John uses a literary motif in his presentation of Jesus' life that highlights
the fact that whenever Jesus said something deeply spiritual, he was inevitably misunderstood: the Jews misunderstand Jesus' reference to the
"temple" (2:20); Nicodemus and new birth (3:4, 9); the woman at the well
and the living water (4:11, 15); the disciples' question about food (4:31); the
people and the bread (6:34, 42, 52); the crowd asks, "Who is trying to kill
you?" (7:20); no one will know where the Christ is from (7:27); the Jews
don't know where Jesus is going (7:35; 8:19, 22); misunderstanding about
the Father (8:27); "How can you say, 'You will become free'?" (8:33); "You've

seen Abraham?" (8:57); the disciples and the good shepherd (10:6); the disciples and Lazarus's sleep (11:12); Martha confused about Lazarus rising again (11:24); God's voice misunderstood (12:28-29); the crowd and Jesus being "lifted up" (12:34); Peter and the foot washing (13:7); Thomas and Jesus' departure (14:5); the disciples and "a little while" (16:17); Jesus' word about John's death (21:23).

14 ON JESUS' LIPS

[1]It is important to note that Matthew uses the same Greek word (*eleos*) to translate the Hebrew word *hesed* as it is most frequently used in the Septuagint.

[2]Another interpretation of this statement is that the phrase "son of man" is being used to mean simply "a person." In that case Jesus is saying that people are masters of the Sabbath, which agrees with a similar saying in Mark 2:27, "The Sabbath was made for man not man for the Sabbath."

17 PAUL AND THE PATH TO REDEMPTION

[1]Compare Matthew 11:30, where the related word *chrēstos* is used to describe Jesus' yoke as "easy" or "kind."

19 HESED IN POST–AD 70 JUDAISM

[1]Avot de Rabbi Nathan 4.1, in *Scholastic Rabbinism: A Literary Study of the Fathers According to Rabbi Nathan* (Providence, RI: Brown Judaic Studies, 1982).

[2]Yerucham Levovitz, in Daniel Z. Feldman, *Divine Footsteps: Chesed and the Jewish Soul*, (New York: Yeshiva University Press, 2008), 2.

20 *GEMILUT HESED* AND *TIKKUN OLAM*

[1]These examples are from Daniel Feldman's remarkable book *Divine Footsteps: Chesed and the Jewish Soul* (New York: Yeshiva University Press, 2008).

[2]David A. Teutsch, *Community, Gemilut Hesed, and Tikun Olam* (Wyncote, PA: Reconstructionist Rabbinical College Press, 2009), 63.

[3]Y. A. Korff, "The Fallacy, Delusion and Myth of Tikkun Olam," Jewish News Syndicate, June 3, 2013, www.jns.org/the-fallacy-delusion-and-myth-of -tikkun-olam.

[4]The finest introduction to hesed in Judaism is Jonathan Sacks's masterful book *To Heal a Fractured World: The Ethics of Responsibility.*

[5]John J. Parsons, "Gemilut Chasadim: Further Thoughts on Parashat Terumah," Hebrew for Christians, www.hebrew4christians.com/Scripture /Parashah/Summaries/Terumah/Chesed/chesed.html.

CONCLUSION: DO JUSTICE, LOVE MERCY, WALK HUMBLY

[1]Bryan Stevenson, *Just Mercy: A Story of Justice and Redemption* (New York: Spiegel & Grau, 2014), 314.

[2]Stevenson, *Just Mercy*, 294.

[3]Frederick Buechner, *Telling the Truth: The Gospel as Tragedy, Comedy, and Fairy Tale* (San Francisco: HarperSanFrancisco, 1977), 98.

AFTERWORD

[1]*Awakenings*, directed by Penny Marshall, screenplay by Steven Zaillian (Columbia Pictures, 1991); based on Oliver Sacks, *Awakenings* (New York: Simon and Schuster, 1973).

BIBLIOGRAPHY

BOOKS

Andrews, Rex B. *What the Bible Teaches About Mercy.* Zion, IL: Zion Faith Homes, 1985.

Barr, James. *The Semantics of Biblical Language.* London: SCM Press, 1983.

Benner, Jeff A. *The Ancient Hebrew Language and Alphabet.* College Station, TX: Virtualbookworm, 2004.

Bentorah, Chaim. *Hebrew Word Study: A Hebrew Teacher's Search for the Heart of God.* Bloomington, IN: WestBow Press, 2012.

Bloch, Abraham P. *The Biblical and Historical Background of Jewish Customs and Ceremonies.* New York: KTAV Publishing House, 1980.

Bonsirven, Joseph. *Palestinian Judaism in the Time of Jesus.* New York: Holt, Rinehart and Winston, 1964.

Botterweck, G. Johannes, and Helmer Ringgren, eds. *Theological Dictionary of the Old Testament,* vol. 5. Grand Rapids: Eerdmans, 1986.

Bowker, John. *The Targums and Rabbinic Literature: An Introduction to Jewish Interpretations of Scripture.* Cambridge: Cambridge University Press, 1969.

Boyd-Taylor, Cameron. "The Semantics of Biblical Language *Redux.*" In *"Translation Is Required": The Septuagint in Retrospect and Prospect,* edited by Robert James Victor Hiebert, 41-58. Atlanta, GA: Society of Biblical Literature, 2010.

Brueggemann, Walter. *The Psalms and the Life of Faith.* Minneapolis: Fortress, 1995.

Budge, E. A. Wallis. *The Gods of the Egyptians: Studies in Egyptian Mythology.* New York: Dover, 1969.

Buxbaum, Yitzhak. *The Life and Teachings of Hillel.* New York: Rowman and Littlefield, 1973.

Chaim, Chafetz. *Ahavath Chesed.* Jerusalem: Feldheim, 1967.

Charlesworth, James H., and Loren L. Johns. *Hillel and Jesus: Comparative Studies of Two Major Religious Leaders.* Minneapolis: Fortress, 1997.

Clark, Gordon R. *The Word "Hesed" in the Hebrew Bible.* Journal for the Study of the Old Testament Supplement Series. Sheffield: Sheffield Academic Press, 1993.

Clark, Maityahu. *Etymological Dictionary of Biblical Hebrew Based on the Commentaries of Samson Raphael Hirsch.* Jerusalem: Feldheim, 1999.

Clines, David J. A. *The Concise Dictionary of Classical Hebrew.* Sheffield: Sheffield Phoenix Press, 2009.

Danby, Herbert, ed. and trans. *The Mishnah.* Oxford: Oxford University Press, 1933.

Feldman, Daniel Z. *Divine Footsteps: Chesed and the Jewish Soul.* New York: Yeshiva University Press, 2008.

Gesenius, William, and Edward Robinson. *A Hebrew and English Lexicon of the Old Testament.* Boston: Edwin Crocker, 1846.

Glueck, Nelson. *Hesed in the Bible.* Eugene, OR: Wipf and Stock, 1967.

Harris, R. Laird, Gleason L. Archer, and Bruce K. Waltke. *Theological Wordbook of the Old Testament.* Chicago: Moody Press, 1980.

Heschel, Abraham Joshua. *I Asked for Wonder: A Spiritual Anthology.* Edited by Samuel H. Dresner. New York: Crossroad, 2001.

Hillebrecht, Mike. *Chesed: Beyond the Veil of Mercy.* Portland, OR: Charis Academy Publishing, 2012.

Jastrow, Marcus. *A Dictionary of the Targumim, the Talmud Babli And Yerushalmi, and the Midrashic Literature.* New York: G. P. Putnam's Sons, 1896.

Kelman, Stuart. *Chesed Shel Emet: The Truest Act of Kindness.* Oakland, CA: EKS Publishing, 2013.

Kidner, Derek. *Psalms: An Introduction and Commentary.* 2 vols. Downers Grove, IL: InterVarsity Press, 1973.

Klein, Ernest. *A Comprehensive Etymological Dictionary of the Hebrew Language for Readers of English.* Jerusalem: Carta, 1987.

Lange, Nicholas de. *The Penguin Dictionary of Judaism.* London: Penguin Books, 2008.

Magness, Jodi, and Seymour Gitin, eds. *Hesed Ve-Emet: Studies in Honor of Ernest S. Frerichs.* Atlanta: Scholars Press, 1998.

Mantel, Hugo. *Studies in the History of the Sanhedrin.* Cambridge, MA: Harvard University Press, 1961.

McWhorter, John H. *The Language Hoax: Why the World Looks the Same in Any Language*. Oxford: Oxford University Press, 2014.

——. *The Story of Human Language*. Audio lecture series. The Great Courses, 2004.

Nouwen, Henri J. M., Donald P. McNeill, and Douglas A. Morrison. *Compassion: A Reflection on the Christian Life*. New York: Doubleday, 1983.

Osborne, Grant. *The Hermeneutical Spiral*. Downers Grove, IL: IVP Academic, 2004.

Oswalt, John. *Hesed: Enduring, Eternal, Undeserved Love*. The Bible Among the Myths. Grand Rapids: Zondervan, 2009.

Oswalt, John, and Dennis F. Kinlaw. *Lectures in Old Testament Theology*. Anderson, IN: Francis Asbury Press, 2010.

Pick, Bernhard. *Jesus in the Talmud: His Personality, His Disciples and His Sayings*. 1913. Reprint, London: Forgotten Books, 2012.

Ruberstein, Jeffrey L. *Rabbinic Stories*. New York: Paulist Press, 2002.

Sacks, Rabbi Jonathan. *To Heal a Fractured World: The Ethics of Responsibility*. New York: Schocken Books, 2005.

Sakenfeld, Katherine Doob. *The Meaning of Hesed in the Hebrew Bible: A New Inquiry*. Eugene, OR: Wipf and Stock, 1978.

Sanders, E. P. *Judaism: Practice and Belief, 63 BC–66 AD*. London: SCM Press, 1992.

Schiffman, Lawence. *Texts and Traditions: A Source Reader for the Study of Second Temple and Rabbinic Judaism*. Hoboken, NJ: KTAV, 1998.

Schlimm, Matthew Richard. *70 Hebrew Words Every Christian Should Know*. Nashville: Abington Press, 2018.

Schneerson, Menachem M. *Garments of the Soul*. New York: Kehot Publishing Society, 2001.

Shapiro, Rabbi Rami. *The Sacred Art of Lovingkindness*. Woodstock, VT: Skylight Paths, 2006.

Silva, Moises. *Biblical Words and Their Meanings*. Grand Rapids: Zondervan, 1983.

Silver, Abba Hillel. *Where Judaism Differed*. Philadelphia: Jewish Publication Society, 1956.

Stevenson, Bryan. *Just Mercy: A Story of Justice and Redemption*. New York: Spiegel & Grau, 2014.

Stuart, D. K. "Steadfast Love." In *The New International Standard Bible Encyclopedia*, edited by Geoffrey W. Bromiley, vol. 4, 613-14. Grand Rapids: Eerdmans, 1988.

Teutsch, David A. *Community, Gemilut Hesed, and Tikkun Olam*. Wyncote, PA: Reconstructionist Rabbinical College Press, 2009.

Waltke, Bruce K. *An Old Testament Theology*. Grand Rapids: Zondervan, 2007.

Walton, John H., Victor H. Matthews, and Mark W. Chavalas. *The IVP Bible Background Commentary: Old Testament*. Downers Grove, IL: IVP Academic, 2000.

Wiesel, Elie. *Messengers of God: Biblical Portraits and Legends*. New York: Summit Books, 1976.

Wolterstorff, Nicholas. *Justice in Love*. Emory University Studies in Law and Religion. Grand Rapids: Eerdmans, 2011.

Young, Brad H. *Meet the Rabbis: Rabbinic Thought and the Teachings of Jesus*. Grand Rapids: Baker Academic, 2007.

Zlotowitz, Meir, trans. *Pirkei Avos: Ethics of the Fathers*. New York: Mesorah Publications, 2002.

JOURNAL ARTICLES

Britt, Brian. "A Literary Approach to the Term Hesed in the Hebrew Bible." *Journal for the Study of the Old Testament* 27, no. 3 (2003): 289-307.

Brueggemann, Walter. "Psalm 109: Three Times 'Steadfast Love.'" *Word and World* 5, no. 2 (1985): 144-54.

Fox, Michael V. "Jeremiah 2:2 and the 'Desert Ideal.'" *The Catholic Biblical Quarterly* 35 (1973): 441-50.

Gentry, Peter J. "Rethinking the Sure Mercies of David in Isaiah 55:3." *Westminster Theological Journal* 69, no. 2 (2007): 280-304.

Korff, Y. A. "The Fallacy, Delusion and Myth of Tikkun Olam." Jewish News Syndicate, June 3, 2013. www.jns.org/the-fallacy-delusion-and-myth-of-tikkun-olam.

Kynes, Will. "God's Grace in the Old Testament: Considering the *Hesed* of the Lord." *Knowing & Doing*, Summer 2010. Available at www.cslewisinstitute.org/webfm_send/430.

Laney, J. Carl. "God's Self-Revelation in Exodus 34:6-8." *Bibliotheca Sacra* 158, no. 629 (2001): 37-51.

Montgomery, James A. "Hebrew *Hesed* and Greek *Charis*." *Harvard Theological Review* 30, no. 2 (1939): 97-102.

Nadel, Sigfried, and Theodore Baker. "The Origins of Music." *The Musical Quarterly* 16, no. 4 (1930): 531-46.

Paldiel, Mordecai. "Hesed and the Holocaust." *Journal of Ecumenical Studies* 23, no. 1 (1986): 90-106.

Perry, Edmund. "The Meaning of *'emuna* in the Old Testament." *Journal of Bible and Religion* 21, no. 4 (1953): 252-56.

Pryor, Dwight A. "Abounding in Hesed." The Center for Judaic-Christian Studies, 2014.

Ramon, Einat. "The Matriarchs and the Torah of Hesed (Lovingkindness)." *Nashim: A Journal of Jewish Women's Studies & Gender Issues* 10, no. 2 (2005): 154-77.

Rosenthal, Gilbert S. "Tikkun ha-Olam: The Metamorphosis of a Concept." *The Journal of Religion* 85, no. 2 (2005): 214-40.

Routledge, Robin. "Hesed as Obligation: A Reexamination." *Tyndale Bulletin* 46, no. 1 (1995): 179-96.

Sakenfeld, Katherine Doob. "The Problem of Divine Forgiveness in Numbers 14." *Catholic Biblical Quarterly* 37, no. 3 (1975): 317-30.

Whitley, C. F. "The Semantic Range of Hesed." *Biblica* 62, no. 4 (1981): 519-26.

UNPUBLISHED THESES

Bell, Bernard. "Ruth: A Hesed Story." Term paper for Dr. Bruce Waltke, Biblical Theology, Spring 1996. Regent College, Vancouver, BC.

Bowen, Boone M. "A Study of Hesed." Dissertation, Graduate School of Yale University, 1938.

Wahl, Loren Otto. "Chesed, God's Unconditional Love and the Resulting Responsibilities of Man." Conservative Baptist Theological Seminary, 1970.

Yarbrough, Glenn. "The Significance of Hesed in the Old Testament." Southern Baptist Theological Seminary, 1949.

VIDEO RESOURCES

A kind tennis player: "Novak Djokovic: Respect for a Ball Boy (French Open)." Published by Manish Yadav, YouTube, February 4, 2017. https://youtu.be/iV2AzllfV9c.

Singing to an elderly woman: "Gladys Wilson and Naomi Feil." Published by memorybridge, YouTube, May 26, 2009. https://youtu.be/CrZXz10FcVM.

A town learns sign language: "An Entire Town Reveals the Most Emotional Surprise to a Hearing-Impaired Resident." Published by Dr. Thais, YouTube, February 23, 2016. https://youtu.be/Kjep4G2OWzc.

An unsung hero: "Street Concert." Published by Thai Life Insurance, YouTube, August 5, 2014. www.youtube.com/watch?v=k0KzquDdSM8.

SCRIPTURE INDEX

ABOUT THE AUTHOR

For many years Michael Card has struggled to listen to Scripture at the level of the imagination. The result has been thirty-seven albums and twenty-seven books, all examining a different element of the Bible, from the life of the apostle Peter to slavery in the New Testament to Christ-centered creativity.

He has a master's degree in biblical studies from Western Kentucky University as well as honorary PhDs in music (Whitfield Seminary) and Christian education (Philadelphia Biblical University).

He lives with his wife, Susan, and their four children in Franklin, Tennessee, where together they pursue racial reconciliation and neighborhood renewal.

www.michaelcard.com

ALSO AVAILABLE FROM

MICHAEL CARD

A Fragile Stone:
The Emotional Life of Simon Peter
978-0-8308-3445-7

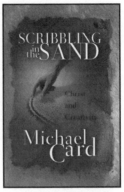

Scribbling in the Sand:
Christ and Creativity
978-0-8308-3254-5

A Better Freedom: Finding Life
as Slaves of Christ (ebook)
978-0-8308-7818-5

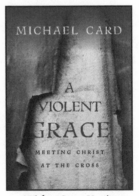

A Violent Grace: Meeting
Christ at the Cross
978-0-8308-3772-4

THE BIBLICAL IMAGINATION SERIES

Matthew: The Gospel of Identity
Mark: The Gospel of Passion
Luke: The Gospel of Amazement
John: The Gospel of Wisdom